The Exciting World of

Creative

Writing

Ruth E. McDaniel

Christian Liberty Press

A publication of

Christian Liberty Press
502 West Euclid Avenue
Arlington Heights, IL 60004
www.christianlibertypress.com

Written by Ruth E. McDaniel
Editing and layout by Edward J. Shewan
Copyediting by Diane C. Olson and Belit M. Shewan
Cover design and layout by Eric D. Bristley
Graphics by Edward J. Shewan

ISBN-13: 978-1-930092-70-9
ISBN-10:   1-930092-70-9

Printed in the United States of America

Contents

Introduction

The Living Webster Encyclopedic Dictionary defines 'writing' as, "to form or inscribe (words) ... a literary composition or production...."

The definition of 'creative' is, "creating ... productive ... inventive ... investing with a new character ... original ... innovative, or imaginative."

So, 'creative writing' would be defined as, "an original, imaginative literary composition or production."

Sounds dull, doesn't it? On the contrary, you're going to find that creative writing is stimulating, inspiring—anything but dull.

Think back to your early childhood when you first began to use your imagination. Life was fun and exciting, even scary, at times. At night, shadows on the wall became giants. Kitchen tables covered with sheets served as tents—perhaps located in the middle of a dangerous African jungle. In an instant, you and your friends were transformed into knights, or ballerinas, or Indians.

Creative writing is the ability to tap into your imagination and write words that make an impact on people's lives, including your own.

This book is designed to help you become a creative writer. Step by step, you'll learn how to use your imagination and skills to write short stories, poetry, prose, novels ... whatever direction you wish to take.

Right now, you're probably saying to yourself, "I could never be a writer." But, I'm going to prove you wrong. If you've ever written a letter, you're already a writer—you just need a little help to make those letters more exciting. Creative writing is nothing more than using your imagination to form stories— or, taking real-life stories and exaggerating them. It's fun and it's easy. All you have to do is put your thoughts on paper and arrange them in an interesting way.

Think of your words as wild horses, and you are the trainer. You're going to learn how to tame your words, bring them under your control, and use them to perform for you. With a little guidance, you'll soon be giving horse shows that will amaze friends and family alike.

Who knows ... you may even decide to submit your work for publication! There is always a need for more Christian writers to help spread God's message throughout the world. Perhaps He'll use you. We'll address that issue in the last chapter.

Now, it's time to gather your "tools" (see Chapter One) and get ready for a great adventure!

Ruth E. McDaniel

Laying the Proper Foundation

Chapter One

Writing Resources

$\mathcal{I}$n every career, there is a need for certain supplies or pieces of equipment. So it is in writing. The following resources will help meet your writing needs.

References for Writers

Before you begin to write creatively, you will need to have your Bible close at hand—for inspiration, guiding principles, and unsurpassed reading material. My Bibles include the *King James Version* and the *New International Version*. I also have *Nave's Topical Bible* in order to locate just the right scripture. Later we will discuss how you can apply Scripture and biblical heroes to modern-day stories.[1]

When it comes to grammar and correct English usage, we will cover a certain amount of language skills in this textbook. For those moments, however, when you are unsure of when to use *was* or *were*, *I* or *me*, *who* or *whom* (etc.), it's wise to keep several basic English textbooks available for reference.[2] *The Elements of Style*, by William Strunk, Jr., and E. B. White, and *Write Right*, by Jan Venolia, are handy references in addition to your basic English grammar books that address the most common writing problems and offer solutions.

What's more, *Webster's Collegiate* or *Roget's Thesaurus* will give you a wide variety of replacement words from which to choose to avoid using the same word too often.[3] This has been called "echoing." Part of creative writing is to make your work flow smoothly with few distractions. If you frequently repeat a word, your readers will find themselves keeping count of that word rather than following your story line.

---

1. In addition, Davis's *Dictionary of the Bible* is indispensable for the Christian writer in understanding biblical terms. Likewise, Berkhof's *Manual of Christian Doctrine* is essential in grasping the teaching of Scripture.
2. Chapman's *Handbook of Grammar and Composition* and Warriner's *English Composition and Grammar* are two excellent resources.
3. Other helpful thesauruses include Sisson's *Synonyms and Word and Expression Locator* and Rodale's *The Synonym Finder*.

Tools of the Trade

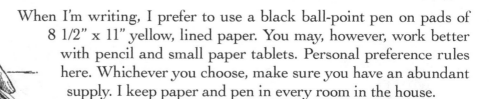

When I'm writing, I prefer to use a black ball-point pen on pads of 8 1/2" x 11" yellow, lined paper. You may, however, work better with pencil and small paper tablets. Personal preference rules here. Whichever you choose, make sure you have an abundant supply. I keep paper and pen in every room in the house.

When a thought or idea strikes, I write it down immediately in my journal. I'm using the term "journal" loosely. Mine happens to be a folder of separate notes. (Remember, I write my thoughts in every room of the house.) Use whatever works best for you … journal, folder, diary, or notebook. As you write daily, you will find that one of these items will fit your needs.

Once you have written your story in longhand, you will need a typewriter, word-processor, or computer. A word-processor or computer will allow you to easily make corrections and store the finished story on a disk. If cost is a factor, however, a typewriter will suffice. A finished manuscript should be typed on 8 1/2" x 11" white bond paper, double-spaced, on one side only, with a one-inch margin all around. Later we'll go into more detail on manuscript preparation.

All right, now that you know what resources to gather, it's time to begin.

Chapter Two

Learn by Reading

In order to become a good writer, you must be a good reader. I don't mean pleasure reading—I mean "study reading."

When you read for pleasure, you skim over the words and absorb only the essentials. When you "study read," you closely examine the way other writers write. Each author has a unique writing style—this is known as a "voice."

The following three examples are excerpts from the Bible, a well-known classic, and a modern-day interpretation of the New Testament written in novel form. Don't just "read" each passage—study the different writing styles. Notice how words are used to describe a particular scene, situation, or person.

Shadrach, Meshach, and Abednego[4]

Daniel 3:19–25

Then Nebuchadnezzar was furious with Shadrach, Meshach, and Abednego, and his attitude toward them changed. He ordered the furnace heated seven times hotter than usual and commanded some of the strongest soldiers in his army to tie up Shadrach, Meshach, and Abednego and throw them into the blazing furnace. So these men, wearing their robes, trousers, turbans, and other clothes, were bound and thrown into the blazing furnace. The king's command was so urgent and the furnace so hot that the flames of the fire killed the soldiers who took up Shadrach, Meshach, and Abednego, and these three men, firmly tied, fell into the blazing furnace.

Then King Nebuchadnezzar leaped to his feet in amazement and asked his advisers, "Weren't there three men that we tied up and threw into the fire?"

They replied, "Certainly, O king."

He said, "Look! I see four men walking around in the fire, unbound and unharmed, and the fourth looks like a son of the gods."

---

4.   Daniel's three friends have refused to bow down to worship King Nebuchadnezzar's gold statue.

Notice how King Nebuchadnezzar reacted: His attitude toward them changed. Then, he ordered his men to heat the furnace seven times hotter than usual. That explains to you, the reader, how enraged the king was—so insanely angry, in fact, that the strongest men in his army were killed from the excess heat.

After Shadrach, Meshach, and Abednego fell into the fiery furnace and were seen walking around unharmed, the writer tells us that Nebuchadnezzar **leaped** to his feet in amazement. That is a wonderfully descriptive action verb. He didn't "get up"—he "leaped" to his feet. Choosing the right word makes the difference between dull and exciting reading.

Oliver Twist[5]

by Charles Dickens

"Oliver!" said Mr. Bumble.

"Yes, sir," replied Oliver, in a low, tremulous voice.

"Pull that cap off your eyes, and hold up your head, sir."

Although Oliver did as he was desired, at once, and passed the back of his unoccupied hand briskly across his eyes, he left a tear in them when he looked up at his conductor. As Mr. Bumble gazed sternly upon him, it rolled down his cheek. It was followed by another, and another. The child made a strong effort, but it was an unsuccessful one. Withdrawing his other hand from Mr. Bumble's, he covered his face with both; and wept until the tears sprung out from between his chin and bony fingers.

"Well!" exclaimed Mr. Bumble, stopping short, and darting at his little charge a look of intense malignity. "Well! Of all the ungratefullest, and worst-disposed boys as ever I see, Oliver, you are the—"

"No, no, sir," sobbed Oliver, clinging to the hand which held the well-known cane; "no, no, sir; I will be good indeed; indeed, indeed I will, sir! I am a very little boy, sir; and it is so— so—"

"So what?" inquired Mr. Bumble in amazement.

"So lonely, sir! So very lonely!" cried the child. "Everybody hates me. Oh! sir, don't pray be cross to me!" The child beat his hand upon his heart; and looked in his companion's face with tears of real agony.

Mr. Bumble regarded Oliver's piteous and helpless look, with some astonishment, for a few seconds; hemmed three or four times in a husky manner; and, after muttering something about "that troublesome cough," bade Oliver dry his eyes and be a good boy. Then once more taking his hand, he walked on with him in silence.

Charles Dickens was a master storyteller who used "show—don't tell!" artfully. Instead of telling us, "Oliver wept uncontrollably," he **showed** us ... Oliver wiped his eyes but still "... left a tear in them when he looked up at [Mr. Bumble]." Under that man's stern gaze, "... it rolled down his cheek ... followed by another ... and another ... until the tears sprung out from between his chin and bony fingers."

---

5. A scene from Chapter Four: Mr. Bumble (a member of the board overlooking the care of the poor and homeless) is taking ten-year-old Oliver to his new position as an undertaker's apprentice.

Can't you picture that poor urchin sobbing his heart out? Do you see how much more effective Dickens's method of "showing" was?

Continuing the story, Oliver hastens to explain his emotional outburst, "... clinging to the hand which held the well-known cane" (this shows us that the boy was afraid of being beaten with the walking cane—there was no need to tell us). Oliver painfully confesses his terrible loneliness, striking his heart with his hand. Even the stern Mr. Bumble was touched.

A well-written story can transport you to another time and place and make you experience what the characters are feeling. That is creative writing.

Men Called Him Master

by Elwyn Allen Smith

Chapter One: A Voice in the Wilderness

"Andrew! The baskets are slipping!" Two men on foot were driving heavily loaded donkeys ahead of them. Across the back of Andrew's tiny beast hung two huge baskets. One slanted crazily forward.

"It ought to hold until we get to the top," answered Andrew. He looked critically at the load and then at the path ahead. They were climbing the bank of a wide gully cut by the floods that rushed down from the barren hills into the valley of the Jordan River every spring. Andrew shouted a command and the donkeys climbed slowly upward. At the top the men stopped to catch their breath.

"John," exclaimed Andrew in disgust, "I have tightened this thing on every hill between Galilee and Judea!" He worked impatiently at the knotted ropes and bound the baskets on the donkey's back. John was not listening. He was gazing at the scene before them.

Torrents of muddy water poured through the gully during the season of rains. Now the clay in the bottom was dry and cracked. Under the hoofs of the animals it was as hard as stone. John pushed his damp hair back from his forehead. His home province, with its green hillsides surrounding the cool Lake of Galilee, was very different from this burnt, rocky land of Judea, which lay southwest of where they stood. The gully carried a sluggish stream of heated air up from the valley; he could feel the damp warmth on his skin. Even on the hilltop there was no cooling breeze.

This story is about the New Testament written in the form of a novel. The beginning sentence catches our attention by using dialogue between Andrew and his brother, John, as they hurry to find John the Baptist.

Immediately, we are drawn into the action. We find ourselves climbing up a steep bank, watching the large baskets teetering on the donkeys' backs. We can almost feel the heat and humidity rising from the valley below. The writer has piqued our interest enough to make us want to turn the page.

Writing Exercise

1. Write one paragraph about someone you know, applying the techniques listed above. Limit the number of adjectives and adverbs. Don't say, "She seems very nervous" or "She shakes, nervously." Instead, **describe** her nervousness: "She blinks, fidgets, and taps one toe on the floor in an irritating way." This is called showing, not telling. Throughout this textbook, I will remind you to "show, not tell." This is one of the most important aspects of writing—so it bears repeating.

Nathan, he runs, jumps, throws, catches, hits, and wrestles. As Nathan goes through the day he laughs and jokes with the people around him. when Nathan is home he plays games, and is never bored with his creative mind.

2. Describe your favorite zoo animal engaged in some action. Make it "come alive" on paper. What does he look like? Smell like? Sound like? Remember, the reader can't see what you're seeing.

A Big eagle soaring with its wings while scouting for food as it grumbles and moans of hunger looks in an open field and finds an adorable hedgehog. The poor little hedgehog squeeks and rolls immediately into its spikey sphere. The eagle squaks with joy as it dives its entire body to the direction of the hedgehog. As the eagle unsheaths its claws out of the corner of its eye sees a massive, scaley snake and goes for that instead.

3. Observe your bedroom as if through the eyes of a stranger. Now, write a complete description of it (and don't forget to include the sounds and scents).

In the room there is a colorful animated photo next to an unmade camouflage bunk bed. There are two windows looking out to the backyard. One of the windows are placed nered to a large wooden dresser, and the other one is next to a tall closet filled with boxes. The main part of the room is a big painting/drafting table.

Chapter Three

Grammar for Writers

*S*ome of the most important skills in today's world are listening, speaking, reading, and writing. Everyday, you're required to communicate your ideas, feelings, and a variety of information. Whether you plan to become a creative writer or not, the way you express yourself will make a dramatic difference in your life.

In this chapter, we will address some basic English skills that will help you become a better communicator by using effective language and organizing your thoughts in a logical way.

Parts of Speech—An Overview

> *A NOUN is a word used as the name of a person, place, animal, substance, measure, object, or quality.*

Persons	Places	Quality	Objects	Substances	Animals	Measures
Phil	school	valor	radio	fire	cat	month
Haitian	store	kindness	nail	oil	mouse	decade
classmate	Maine	attribute	blouse	coal	whale	cup
brother	zoo	ambition	sofa	metal	horse	yard

Examples: The *poet* gave a *reading*.   The *boy* is playing *soccer*.   My *father* cut the *grass*.

Proper Nouns	Common Nouns		
Janet (person)	ship (object)	inch (measure)	lawyer (person)
America (place)	faith (quality)	key (object)	sweetness (quality)
Charles (person)	church (place)	house (place)	food (substance)

NOTE: *Proper* nouns are capitalized (e.g., Janet); *Common* nouns are not capitalized (e.g., ship).

Writing Exercises

Fill in the type of noun from the above list for each of the following words. Is it a *person*, *place*, *animal*, *substance*, *measure*, *object*, or *quality*?

water	*substance*	ocean	*place*	Robert	*person*
mile	*measure*	bear	*animal*	sweetness	*quality*
air	*substance*	building	*place*	kilometer	*measure*
year	*measure*	foot	*measure*	iron	*substance*
book	*object*	courage	*quality*	diamond	*substance*

> **A PRONOUN** *is a word that takes the place of a noun.*

Without pronouns, you would have to use nouns over and over. So, to avoid repetition (i.e., "Ruth is sitting at Ruth's word processor using Ruth's paper."), we substitute another part of speech.

The following are the most commonly used pronouns.

I	my	mine	me	we	he
our	ours	us	myself	ourselves	his
you	your	yours	yourself	yourselves	him
herself	it	its	itself	they	she
their	theirs	them	themselves	what	her
who	whose	whom	this	that	hers
each	these	those	all	any	both
either	neither	few	many	anyone	none
some	one	other	another	anybody	everybody
nobody	somebody	no one	someone	everyone	whoever

Examples: Mary let <u>her</u> cat outside because <u>it</u> was howling.

The boy rode <u>his</u> bike to <u>his</u> friend's house.

Joanne, did <u>you</u> finish <u>your</u> homework?

<u>It</u> doesn't get any better than <u>this</u>.

<u>What</u> kind of movies do <u>you</u> like?

Is <u>everyone</u> happy with <u>his</u> gift?

Writing Exercise

Write ten interesting sentences using a variety of pronouns from the list on the previous page.

1. neither myself nor my friends own a cat.
2. both me and my sister love video games.
3. I cannot wait until it is four o'clock.
4. me, myself, and I are my favorite people.
5. who is your favorite child mom?
6. I did not like eating kale.
7. either I'm crazy or I just saw a bear.
8. my sister is going into the military.
9. no one I know owns a bird.
10. everybody on earth can breathe.

An *ADJECTIVE* is a word used to modify a noun or pronoun.

Adjectives are meant to be descriptive and often answer the questions: *What kind? What color? Which one? How much? How many?*

What kind/color?	Which one?	How much/many?
bright blue eyes	*that* scarf	*several* dollars
violent storm	*this* month	*twenty* cents
famous writers	*last* year	*one* time
used books	*those* donuts	*no* work

Writing Exercise

1. Identify and underline the adjectives below. Fill in the blanks with the most appropriate question: What kind? What color? Which one? How much? How many?

Example: *tiny* airplane   (*What kind?*)

large animals	*what kind*	good company	*what kind*
blue car	*what color*	wide smile	*what kind*
busy city	*what kind*	that style	*which one*
frail woman	*what kind*	fifty pennies	*how many*
brave soldier	*what kind*	biggest banana	*what kind*
tardy employee	*which one*	those earrings	*which one*
first year	*which one*	whole thing	*how much*

2. Write your own adjectives on the blank spaces below to fit the applicable questions.

Example: *big* lake   (*What kind?*)

best	radio	(Which one?)	*twelve*	stars	(How many?)
five	man	(How many?)	*fast*	weeks	(What kind?)
ugly	dress	(What kind?)	*fifteen*	Englishmen	(How many?)
pretty	flowers	(Which one?)	*red*	rose	(What color?)
three	fish	(How many?)	*eight*	dollars	(How much?)
rain	clouds	(What kind?)	*good*	weather	(What kind?)
Nike	shoes	(Which one?)	*big*	house	(Which one?)

> **A VERB is a word that expresses action or otherwise helps to make a statement.**

The *verb* is the only part of speech that can make a statement about a subject.

Example: "Jesus <u>wept</u>." (John 11:35)

No sentence is complete without a verb—not even the shortest sentence. [**Jesus** is the subject; **wept** is the verb.] There are two types of verbs: *action* and *linking* verbs.

The action verb can express either physical or mental action.

Examples: The boy *ran* home.   They *believe* in prayer.

She *calculated* the tax due.   Let's *follow* his advice.

Can you *imagine* such a thing?   *Listen* to the rain.

She *jumped* over the crack.   Susan *finished* her ice cream.

Other verbs help to make a statement by *linking* the **subject** (the part of the sentence about which something is being said) and the **predicate** (the part of the sentence which says something about the subject). One of the most important verbs in this group is: **to be**. The common forms of **to be** are: *is, are, was,* and *were*.

Examples: My brother *is* tall   The apples *are* ripe.

Everything *was* wet.   The people *were* happy.

Writing Exercise

Write ten simple sentences using both action and linking verbs.

1. My mom is going to shop.
2. We are all doing great.
3. Why does he not have to do anything?
4. What is your major in college?
5. My least favorite thing to do is read.
6. My favorite shbuect in school is science.
7. I love anything that has to do with animals.
8. The movie Big Hero Six is my favorite.
9. I used to play basketball and soccer.
10. I can't wait until Rise of Iron comes out.

> An **ADVERB** *is a word used to modify a verb, an adjective, or another adverb.*

The adverb answers the questions: *When? Where? How? To what extent—how much?* or *how long?*

Examples: Set the table **now**. (When?)   Weeds grow **everywhere**. (Where?)

The rain fell **down**. (Where?)   He **recently** visited us. (When?)

She laughed **happily**. (How?)   She danced **gracefully**. (How?)

Here I am. (Where?)   The summer seems **far** away. (To what extent?)

He ran **quickly**. (How?)   The snow fell **endlessly**. (To what extent?)

Writing Exercise

1. Identify the question these adverbs answer.

   (*When? Where? How? To what extent?—how much? or how long?*)

2. Provide an appropriate verb.

Example:

Verb	Adverb	Question
ran	*fast*	*How?*

Verb	Adverb	Question
asked	frequently	How?
talked	wordlessly	How?
rush	there	where
eating	soon	when
jogging	almost	howlong
wrestling	today	when
going	faster	How

Verb	Adverb	Question
flying	forever	how long
jumping	up	where
skipping	promptly	How
going	daily	when
throwing	nearby	where
hopped	suddenly	when
walked	slowly	How

> *A PREPOSITION is a word used to show the relationship of a noun or pronoun to some other word in a sentence.*

The following is a list of words that are the most common prepositions:

about	because of	during	of	to
above	before	except	off	toward
according to	behind	for	on	under
across	below	from	on account of	underneath
after	beneath	in	out of	until
against	beside	inside	outside	unto
along	between	in spite of	over	up
among	beyond	instead of	past	upon
around	but	into	since	with
as	by	like	through	within
at	down	near	throughout	without

Writing Exercise

Underline the prepositions that appear in the following sentences and enclose in parentheses the words or phrase that each preposition introduces.

Example: <u>In</u> (American history), there were many great orators.

1. He walked <u>toward</u> (the sun).

2. His foot was caught <u>between</u> (two boards).

3. The man <u>at</u> (the door) is waiting.

4. There was a hot dog stand <u>across</u> (the street).

5. The letter was sent <u>by</u> (express mail).

6. The swords hanging <u>over</u> (the fireplace) were rusty.

7. It snowed <u>throughout</u> (the night).

8. The kitten hid <u>under</u> (the table).

9. Rex ran <u>out</u> (of the house) without his leash.

10. John was nervous <u>during</u> (the exam).

> *A CONJUNCTION is a word used to connect*
> *words or groups of words in a sentence.*

The three most common conjunctions are *and*, *but*, and *or*.

1. *Conjunctions* join single words:

    Examples: Bread *and* butter are delicious with soup.

    Would you rather have tea *or* cocoa?

    The house is small *but* comfortable.

2. *Conjunctions* join groups of words:

    Examples: She galloped over the river *and* through the woods.

    The sheriff wanted to call her *but* had to wait.

    Wolves run in packs *or* wander alone.

3. *Conjunctions* join two independent clauses.[6]

Examples: One sister had ruddy skin, *and* the other sister had a fair complexion.

Chrissy wanted a new doll, *but* she had to wait for her birthday.

We can fly to Arizona, *or* we can drive.

Additional conjunctions are: *nor, for, because, yet, either … or, neither … nor, both … and,* and *not only … but also.*

Examples: We can listen to *either* classical music *or* jazz.

Both John *and* Sally were late.

Not only the monkeys *but also* the elephants enjoy entertaining people.

We waited until closing time, *for* we didn't want to miss a thing.

Writing Exercise

Write three sentences for each of the following conjunctions for a total of twenty-one sentences. Use *and, but, or, yet, neither … nor, not only … but also,* and *because.*

1. My sister and I are playing video games,
2. I love this house, but not the state.
3. I will take ice cream, or cookies.
4. I am not old, yet I don't like to exercise.
5. I like neither beef, nor chicken.
6. Not only do I run, but also jog.
7. I like video games, because I am good at them.
8. Just kidding, I like chicken and beef.
9. I like christmas, but I also like thanksgiving.
10. Do you want to eat chicken or beef,
11. I am not a vegan, yet I don't eat meat.
12. I neither like vegans, nor vegitarians.
13. Not only are vegans dumb, but also skinny.

---

6.   Please note that a *comma* is needed following the first independent clause and before the *conjunction.*

14. I am not a vegin, because I um smart.
15. I take milk and sugar in my coffee.
16. I perfer tea, but he likes coffee.
17. Would you perfer coffee or tea.
18. neither coffee nor tea is good.
19. not only am I a coffee drinker, but also a tea drinker.
20. I drink tea, yet I like coffee better.
21. I like tea because coffee is too sweet.

> **An INTERJECTION is a word used to express strong feeling or sudden emotion and is not related grammatically to other words in the sentence.**

These are short exclamations and are followed by an exclamation point[!]. Interjections are especially important to creative writing because they **spice up** your story. Here are some examples: *Behold! Wow! Hey! Oh! Ah! Well! Whew! Ouch! Alas! Listen! No! Bravo!*

Example: *"Oh!* You frightened me!"

Writing Exercise

Write eight sentences using the interjections listed above or choosing ones of your own.

1. Hey! I know you from some where.
2. Oh! I wasn't expecting you.
3. Ah! well now I understand.
4. Well! That wasn't very nice.
5. Alas! I have found the treasure
6. whew! That was a close one.
7. Listen! You need to pay attention to me.
8. Bravo! That was a great performance.

Summary

Parts of Speech	Use	Examples
Noun	Names	George, store, England, ball
Pronoun	Takes the place of a noun	I, you, me, yourself, it, they, what, who, any, several, anyone, everyone
Adjective	Modifies a noun or pronoun	bright, red, violent, used, last, those, twenty
Verb	Expresses action or helps to make a statement	run, climb, think, plan, follow, was, were, are, feel, touch, write
Adverb	Modifies a verb, an adjective, or another adverb	now, here, very, recently, suddenly, too, daily, faster, brightly, truly
Preposition	Shows the relationship of a noun or pronoun to some other word	in (this world), across (the street), for (Mary), without (her)
Conjunction	Joins words or clauses	and, but, or, nor, for, yet, either ... or.
Interjection	Expresses strong feeling or sudden emotion	Wow! Oh! Ah! Well! Whew! Wait! Now! No!

Note: The same word can function as a *noun* or a *verb*, as an *adverb* or a *preposition*, or as a *pronoun* or an *adjective*, depending on how it is used.

Examples: I marked the *date* on the calendar. (noun)

I don't want to *date* Sally's brother. (verb)

My sister tagged *along* with us. (adverb)

We gathered wild flowers that grew *along* the road. (preposition)

Both did their homework. (pronoun)

Both boys played ball. (adjective)

Chapter Four

Complete the Thought

$\mathcal{N}$ow that you have identified the eight parts of speech, it is time to put words together in such a way that they express a complete thought—this is known as a *sentence*.

Examples: The lonely boy. (incomplete sentence)

Everyone in the van. (incomplete sentence)

Up the hillside. (incomplete sentence)

These three groups of words are not sentences because they do not express complete thoughts.

A complete sentence must have a *subject* and a *predicate* (we referred to these terms in Chapter Three under *linking verb*).

- The **subject** is the part of the sentence about which something is being said.
- The **predicate** is the part of the sentence which says something about the subject.

Let's finish the incomplete sentences shown above.

The Subjects	The Predicates
The lonely boy	wanted a friend.
Everyone in the van	sang loudly.
The goats	climbed up the hillside.

You can see what a difference complete sentences make. Sentences don't have to be long to be complete.

Examples: Birds fly.   Babies cry.   Dogs bark.

While these three examples are complete sentences, they are neither very descriptive nor very interesting. In order to write creatively, you must be able to put sentences together in a way that (you hope) entertains and informs. Regardless, sentences must contain both subjects and predicates.

Writing Exercise

The following groups of words are a mixture of complete and incomplete sentences. Place a period at the end of each complete sentence, and add more words to make the unfinished sentences complete.

1. Donna thought of _____

2. Everywhere I go _____

3. He closed the door _____

4. The yellow raincoat _____

5. English grammar is tedious _____

6. My car starts _____

7. We stopped for lunch _____

8. Singing in the rain _____

9. Was watched closely _____

10. Opening next week _____

Punctuation

In written language, punctuation is used to indicate pauses, stops, questions, and quotations, etc.

- A *period* [.] follows a statement and is also used for abbreviations (a.m., Mr., etc.).

  Examples: The child had curly hair.   10:30 a.m.

- A *question mark* [?] follows a question.

  Example: Where are my keys?

- An *exclamation point* [!] follows an exclamation. (Remember the interjection.)

  Example: Whoa! What a ride!

- A *colon* [:] precedes a list of words, examples, and sentences that are formally introduced. Colons normally follow words like *the following, as follows, as these,* and *given below.* Colons are also used after formal salutations, in telling time to separate the hour from the minutes, and in citing Bible verses.

  Examples: The ingredients are as follows: two eggs, one cup milk, four cups flour, and one-half cup sugar.

  Dear Mrs. Smith: It is now 3:16 p.m.   Deuteronomy 6:4–9

❦ A *semicolon* [;] signals a pause stronger than a comma but not as strong as a period. It is also used between independent clauses in a sentence if they are not joined by *and, but, or, nor, for, yet.*

Example: Volunteers were called; many came forward.

Note: A semicolon is used, however, before a conjunction if the two clauses contain commas within themselves (*See example below.*)

Example: Singers, dancers, musicians, and workers were needed; but only singers, dancers, and musicians applied.

❦ A *comma* [,] is used to separate items in a series, phrases, clauses, and interjections; they are also used with terms of direct address and dates.

Examples: We can walk, ride, or take the train.

Yes, it's a lovely day.

"I'm sorry," Mrs. Smith said.

Running as fast as he could, Roger caught the bus.

Sara watched the sunset, and she felt content.

Have you seen our garden, Mr. Jones?

To tell the truth, I didn't like it.

On April 15, 1995, the store opened for business.

❦ *Quotation marks* [" "] are used to enclose the words of a speaker; titles of articles, poems, and stories; or to indicate an unusual use of a word.

Examples: "We must try to get along," said Reverend Jones.

Joyce Kilmer's "Trees" is a well-known poem.

John's "castle" was little more than a shack.

❦ An *apostrophe* ['] is used with an "s" to form the possessive of a singular noun. Plural nouns ending in "s" only need the apostrophe. Other plural nouns need an apostrophe and "s."

Examples: The boy's jacket   The ladies' hats   The children's picnic   Chris's car

Note: See "Contraction" below for additional uses of the apostrophe.

❦ A *hyphen* [-] is used when writing compound numbers, to divide a word at the end of a line, with fractions used as adjectives, and in an adjective made up of two or more words.

Examples: Twenty-four hours (compound numbers)

The job was for volun-

teers. (word divided at the end of a line)

One-third cup (fractions used as adjectives)

Well-to-do gentlemen (adjectives made up of 2-3 words)

Up-to-date information (adjectives made up of 2-3 words)

Summary of Punctuation Marks

Name	Symbol	Function
Period	.	follows a complete thought or statement
Question Mark	?	follows a question
Exclamation Point	!	follows an exclamation or interjection
Colon	:	precedes lists, separates hour and minutes
Semicolon	;	signals strong pause
Comma	,	separates words, phrases, clauses
Quotation Marks	" "	encloses quotations, titles, etc.
Apostrophe	'	shows possession
Hyphen	-	connects words, divides words at end of line

Writing Exercise

Provide the correct punctuation for each of the following sentences. All of the marks of punctuation listed above will be needed. Each sentence may require several.

1. The girls teacher gave them one third cup of sugar to complete their recipes

2. Some of us were ready several were not

3. The time was 12 45 p m and only twenty three people were present

4. Okay Mrs Jones said that is what we will do

5. Wow That was great

6. His ship turned out to be a canoe

7. The Gettysburg Address by Abraham Lincoln is well known by most Americans

8. Stop said the grocer I forgot to put your bread in the bag

9. Sally thought the boss   voice sounded angry

10. One half of her receipts went to Bess   account

11. The schedule is as follows open at 9 00 a m lunch at 12 00 noon and close at 5 00 p m

12. She wanted to attend the carnival picnic and concert I preferred the theater

13. The lions eyes glowed in the dark

14. Three fifths of the treasure was made up of gold diamonds silver and rubies

15. Home by Edgar A. Guest is one of my favorite poems

> **A CONTRACTION is a word made by combining or shortening two words.**

An apostrophe takes the place of the letters that are omitted.

Examples: *She is* correct.   *She's* correct.

We will be there.   *We'll* be there.

They *could not* come.   They *couldn't* come.

In creative writing, you'll want to sound as natural as possible. Listen to people conversing. Most conversations include contractions. Otherwise, they would sound too stiff and formal.

Formal: *"There is* Sally.

She is my best friend.

When *we are* together, *it is* always exciting and fun."

Informal: *"There's* Sally.

She's my best friend.

When *we're* together, *it's* always exciting and fun."

Which example sounds more natural to you? (I hope you chose the informal examples above.) If you heard someone speaking in formal sentences, you'd wonder why he was talking that way. You certainly wouldn't enjoy reading a story written in such a formal tone. So, remember contractions when you begin to write, but be careful not to overuse these handy devices.

List of Common Contractions

I am	➡ I'm	is not	➡	isn't
I would	➡ I'd	you would	➡	you'd
you are	➡ you're	let us	➡	let's
he is	➡ he's	does not	➡	doesn't
we are	➡ we're	do not	➡	don't
they are	➡ they're	who is	➡	who's
she is	➡ she's	there have	➡	there've
you will	➡ you'll	would have	➡	would've
she would	➡ she'd	could have	➡	could've
it is	➡ it's	will not	➡	won't
are not	➡ aren't	cannot	➡	can't
were not	➡ weren't	should not	➡	shouldn't
has not	➡ hasn't	had not	➡	hadn't

Writing Exercise

Rewrite the paragraph below using contractions to make it sound more natural.

Sometimes I take my little sister shopping with me, although I do not always have the time. My sister enjoys shopping with me and I am glad when she is able to come along. It is fun taking her with me. I cannot think of one shopping trip that has not been successful. I am glad she will remember our times together when she is older. Maybe she will take me shopping with *her* some day. It has been wonderful.

_____

_____

_____

_____

_____

_____

_____

_____

_____

_____

_____

_____

_____

_____

Chapter Five

Forming Paragraphs

In previous chapters, we briefly covered the eight parts of speech, composition, and complete sentences. Now we need to look more closely at the contents of those sentences, which include **phrases** and **participles**. Then, we'll combine sentences into **paragraphs**.

Let's start by reviewing three important types of phrases that frequently work their way into creative writing: *similes*, *metaphors*, and *clichés*.

> **A SIMILE is a figure of speech which compares two unlike things.**

This phrase is often preceded by *like* or *as*.

Examples: runs *like* the wind   pretty *as* a picture   hungry *as* a bear

cheeks *like* roses   flat *as* a pancake   ugly *as* a dog

Similes can add color and vivid mental images to your writing, but only if used sparingly—and if they're fresh.

Writing Exercise

Create five of your own original similes (comparisons)

Examples: Writes *like* a "word-warrior"

shines *like* a newborn baby's eyes

hot *as* an Arizona rock at high noon

1. _____

2. _____

3. _____

4. _____

5. _____

> **A METAPHOR** *is a figure of speech in which a word or phrase claims to be another dissimilar object.*

The difference between a *simile* and a *metaphor* is that a simile suggests one thing is *like* another—a metaphor states one thing *is* something else.

Examples: all the world's a stage

the ship plows the sea

computers have senses and a memory

> **A CLICHÉ** *is a phrase or expression made trite and commonplace by overuse.*

Unlike *similes* and *metaphors*, which add liveliness and depth to your writing, you'll want to avoid these worn-out phrases "like the plague," since they'll only dull your style.

hot as a firecracker	good as gold	better late than never
burn the midnight oil	busy as a bee	let's face it
the weaker sex	few and far between	without rhyme or reason
needless to say	in the nick of time	Mother Nature
on the ball	nipped in the bud	too funny for words
sweat of his brow	cool as a cucumber	strong as an ox
through thick and thin	quick as a flash	all things being equal
lose your head	white as a sheet	don't rock the boat
the whole ball of wax	sitting on a time bomb	sharp as a tack
food for thought	bump on a log	a diamond in the rough
apple of his eye	method to his madness	cold as ice
old Father Time	ripe old age	high on the hog

There are many more, but I think you get the idea.

If you include timeworn phrases in your sentences, readers will lose interest in your piece. Today's reader demands fresh and creative writing.

Writing Exercise

Create five original metaphors by finishing the following sentences with an unlike comparison:

Examples: Joy is a warm bed on a cold night.

Poetry is a bouquet of flowers in a desert.

1.   Beauty is _____

2.   The sun is _____

3.   The stars are _____

4.   A mother is _____

5.   Words are _____

Verb Form	Participle (Functions as an *Adjective*)
singing	singing tires
working	working women
eating	eating habits
following	the following night
punishing	punishing rain
running	running water
sleeping	sleeping children

> *A PARTICIPLE is a verb form used as an adjective.*

🐿 A **present participle** always ends in *-ing*. (See the *participle* column above for examples.)

🐿 A **past participle** usually ends in *-ed, -d, -t, -n,* or *-en*: bitten, surprised, thrown, etc.

🐿 A **perfect participle** is always formed by prefixing the word *having* to the past participle: *having* bitten, *having* surprised, *having* thrown.

🐿 A **participial phrase** is a group of words in which a participle introduces related words that act together as an adjective. The following italicized examples are participial phrases.

Examples: *Running down the road,* I saw a deer.

Surprised at the large attendance, Sally hurried to the podium.

Jumping from stone to stone, Andy soon grew tired.

Having seen the movie, I didn't recommend it.

A DANGLING PARTICIPIAL PHRASE is
a phrase that does not sensibly modify the subject
of the sentence.

When the appropriate subject is missing, the phrase *dangles*, causing the sentence to sound foolish or even humorous. This is a common mistake in speaking and writing and can be corrected by inserting the proper subject and rewriting the sentence.

Incorrect:	Having stopped for soda, the excursion continued. (Who stopped?)
Correct:	Having stopped for soda, we continued the excursion.
Incorrect:	Walking through the park, a statue suddenly appeared. (Who walked?)
Correct:	Walking through the park, we saw a statue suddenly appear.

A MISPLACED MODIFIER is a modifier that is
inserted in the wrong part of the sentence.

When a participle modifies the proper word but is *misplaced*, the meaning is confused. All of the right words are there—you just need to rearrange them in the proper order.

Incorrect:	I placed the jar in the refrigerator *with the broken lid*.
Correct:	I placed the jar *with the broken lid* in the refrigerator.
Incorrect:	I left my wallet on the table *containing money and credit cards*.
Correct:	I left my wallet *containing money and credit cards* on the table.

Conclusion: Review your sentences carefully to make sure they say what you want them to say. Place your words and phrases in proper order, and don't 'misplace' or 'dangle' your participles and modifiers.

Writing Exercise

None of the following sentences make sense. Rewrite and rearrange them until they sound logical.

1. Having washed the clothes, the clothesline was quickly filled up.

2. The lake was, driving past, calm and peaceful.

3. Sleeping in the sun, a bee bothered the man.

   _____

4. Enchanted by their beauty, a bouquet of flowers was picked.

   _____

5. Jumping into the lake, the ball was retrieved by the dog.

   _____

6. I laid the silverware on the table with the gold initials.

   _____

7. She preferred the dress in the store with the polka-dots.

   _____

8. Running through the park, a fountain sprayed me.

   _____

9. I found the book returning to the library.

   _____

10. Watching the sunrise, a bird flew overhead.

   _____

> **A PARAGRAPH consists of one or more complete sentences containing the same topic.**

Just as a sentence is a group of words expressing a complete thought, a paragraph consists of one or more complete sentences containing the same topic. The "rule" is: *each paragraph must deal with a single theme*.

The first sentence normally states the main idea. The balance of the paragraph contains sentences that support and develop that theme. In a long paragraph, the final sentence summarizes the preceding sentences. However, there's a great deal of flexibility allowed in writing paragraphs. Writers are free to express themselves in their own way as long as they follow the one-topic-per-paragraph rule.

The following are the first two paragraphs from an article I wrote for *Senior Circuit Newspaper* entitled, "The Story of Old Glory" (published July 1, 1993):

The Story of Old Glory

by Ruth E. McDaniel

On June 14, 1777, the Continental Congress resolved that "the flag of the United States shall have thirteen stripes, alternating red and white, with a union of thirteen stars of white on a field of blue...." The stars and stripes each symbolized the original thirteen colonies. The official announcement was made September 3, 1777. Despite popular belief, there is no documentary evidence to support the story that Betsy Ross made the first American flag, as asserted by her grandson, William J. Canby, on March 14, 1870.

In 1794, Congress voted to add two stripes and two stars to the flag in recognition of the admission of Vermont and Kentucky to the Union, and to continue that pattern in the future. However, as the country expanded, it became unfeasible to keep adding stars and stripes for each admitted state. So, in 1818 Congress voted to return to the seven red stripes alternating with six white stripes, representing the original colonies. They would continue to add one star for each state as it was admitted to the Union. A star for Hawaii, our fiftieth state, was the most recent addition on July 4, 1960.

Note: The first paragraph describes the creation of the American flag (ending with an interesting little side-note). I started a new paragraph to discuss the change in the flag in 1794. The rest of the second paragraph supports that theme.

The next example is an excerpt from a short fiction story I wrote for *Short Stuff Magazine* entitled "Thanksgiving Dinner" (published November 26, 1994):

Thanksgiving Dinner

by Ruth E. McDaniel

Ruben couldn't remember ever having a more difficult task. Oh, he had killed chickens before. You can't live on a farm all your life and not have to kill chickens. But, this was different. Dudley wasn't a dumb old chicken—in fact, he wasn't a chicken at all—he was probably the smartest duck that ever lived! Well, at any rate, he was the biggest, healthiest duck Ruben had ever seen, and he wasn't stupid, either.

Ruben remembered when Dudley was hatched. Ruben held the little, squirming, fuzzy thing in the palm of his hand, and he felt a bond forming.

Note: In writing fiction, it is important to begin your story with a sentence that piques your reader's interest. That's known as a "grabber" (we'll address that topic in Chapter Twelve). So, because this was a fiction story and not a nonfiction article, the first sentence wasn't "informational" as it was in the preceding excerpt. However, I followed the "rule" and started a new paragraph when a new subject was introduced (Ruben thought back to the day Dudley was hatched).

Summary

Each paragraph should contain one or more complete sentences expressing the same thought, idea, or theme. It may include an introductory (first) sentence and a summarizing (last) sentence. A new paragraph is called for when the thought, idea, or theme changes.

Also try to arrange the sentences within your paragraphs in proper order according to their time or importance. It's confusing to your readers if you scramble the information you are giving them.

Writing Exercise

Choose two of the topics listed below and write, in the space provided, one paragraph for each (including at least five sentences). Remember to stick to the same main idea and put your sentences in proper order. Use a simile or metaphor if appropriate, but please—no clichés!

Note: Vary the lengths of your sentences. Paragraphs filled with sentences of the same length are boring. To retain a reader's interest, however, you should include sentences ranging from two to twenty words. (A twenty-word sentence is usually a compound-complex sentence joined by a *conjunction*, a *comma*, or a *semicolon*.) In general, keep your sentences to a length of twenty words or less, unless you are an experienced writer. In addition, do not forget to use a few *contractions* (terms that use an apostrophe to take the place of omitted letters or numbers) to make your sentences sound less formal.

Topics to Choose From:

1. Computers are helpful.
2. Basketball is fun.
3. The Bible has great stories.
4. Housekeeping is necessary.
5. Astronauts have fascinating jobs.
6. Dogs are good companions.
7. Daily prayer is important.
8. Hiking is good exercise.
9. Flowers even grow in the desert.
10. Friendships are special.

Paragraph One

_____

_____

_____

_____

_____

_____

_____

_____

_____

_____

_____

_____

Paragraph Two

_____

_____

_____

_____

_____

_____

_____

_____

_____

_____

_____

Chapter Six

Writing Creatively

$\mathcal{I}$n this chapter, we'll review the three most common forms of creative writing: *poetry*, *prose*, and *fiction*.

Poetry

Poetry has been described as art in written form. Just as an artist creates a picture for the eye, a poet creates a word-picture for the heart.

> **A POEM is a composition in verse.**

Through a few well-chosen words, the poet describes an emotion, person, place, sight, sound, taste, touch, etc. Those words can be expressed through *free verse* (contemporary) poetry or *traditional* (rhythm and rhyme) poetry. Regardless of the form or pattern you use to convey your thoughts, the idea is to elicit an emotional response from your reader.

Reading good poetry is the best way to learn how to write good poetry. Did you know that the Bible is filled with beautiful poetry? The following is written in free verse form:

Examples: The Lord is my shepherd; I shall not want.

He maketh me to lie down in green pastures:

he leadeth me beside the still waters.

He restoreth my soul....—Psalm 23:1–3

Our Father which art in heaven,

Hallowed be thy name. Thy kingdom come.

Thy will be done in earth,

as it is in heaven.—Matthew 6:9–10

The entire book of Lamentations consists of free verse poetry:

Examples: How lonely sits the city

that was full of people!

How like a widow is she,[7]

who was great among the nations!

The princess among the provinces

has become a slave![8]—Lamentations 1:1 (NKJV)

(*Remember your Creator*) e'er the silver cord be loosed,

or the golden bowl be broken,

or the pitcher be broken at the fountain,

or the wheel broken at the cistern.

Then shall the dust return to the earth as it was:

and the spirit shall return unto God who gave it.—Ecclesiastes 12:6–7

Poetical Devices

Poets use a variety of devices to invigorate their poetry.

- An *acrostic* uses the first letter of each line to form a word, name, or message:

    Example: **R** uns like the wind

    U nder sunny skies and

    T hanks the Lord for

    H ealth and happiness

- An *allegory* is a story or poem in which people, things, and happenings have another meaning (as in fables and parables) for didactic or explanatory purposes. For example, the tortoise and the hare were personified to prove that speed doesn't always win the race.

- *Alliteration* is repeating the same consonant sound, especially in initial stressed syllables ("**S**am **s**aw **S**ally in the **s**un.").

- *Assonance* uses identical vowel sounds in several words ("For the l**o**ve **o**f a d**o**ve …").

- *Consonance* uses identical consonant sounds in a harmony of tones (**rh**yme-**r**oam-**r**eam; **bl**ack-**bl**ow-**bl**iss).

---

7. The author used a simile. He compares the city of Jerusalem to a widow.

8. The author used a metaphor. He claims that Jerusalem, once a princess, has now become a slave.

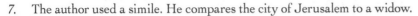

- *Internal rhyme* uses rhyming within a line ("The little **boy** was such a **joy**.").

- A *metaphor* states that one thing is another dissimilar thing. (The words **like** and **as** are not used.)

- A *narrative poem* is a poem that tells a story.

- An *onomatopoeia* (pronounced: on´-a-mot´-a-pee´-a) is a word that imitates a sound (bang, boom, ding-dong, crack, slam, honk, whoosh, crash).

- An *oxymoron* (pronounced: ocks´-ee-more´-on) uses contradiction to emphasize a point (a joyful sadness; a loud silence; a wise fool).

- A *parody* is a literary or musical work that imitates a famous poem, story, or song in a humorous, often ridiculing or satirical way.

- *Personification* is a figure of speech (a type of metaphor) that compares a thing, quality, or idea to a person ("The wind was crying"); also, a person or thing thought of as representing (or symbolizing) some quality, thing, or idea ("That woman personifies motherhood.").

- A *refrain* repeats a line or group of lines at certain points in a poem, especially at the end of a stanza.

- A *response poem* is a poem that is seemingly in response to a classic or famous poem—as if answering a question or taking the poem past the original ending.

- *Sight rhyme* uses two or more words which end in identical spelling but do not necessarily rhyme (although, enough, through, tough).

- A *simile* compares one thing to another unlike thing (uses *like* or *as* in the description: "cheeks like roses," "cute as a button").

- *Slant* or *wrenched rhyme* uses words that do not quite rhyme (when, again, then, begin).

A Rhyme

by William Shakespeare

Among the traditional poets is William Shakespeare (1564–1616). In the following verse, Shakespeare uses the poetical device of *personification* by giving the wind such human qualities as unkindness and rudeness, and human features as teeth and breath. Notice that the first two lines end with *sight rhyme*.

Blow, blow thou winter wind,

Thou art not so unkind

   As man's ingratitude;

Thy tooth is not so keen,

Because thou art not seen,

   Although thy breath be rude.

In 1895, Edgar A. Guest (1881–1959) wrote a column in the *Detroit Free Press*, and his simple verse won him a wide audience. The following is an excerpt from one of my favorites:

It Couldn't Be Done

by Edgar A. Guest

Somebody said that it couldn't be done,

But he with a chuckle replied

That "maybe it couldn't," but he would be one

Who wouldn't say so till he'd tried.

So, he buckled right in with the trace of a grin

On his face. If he worried he hid it.

He started to sing as he tackled the thing

That couldn't be done, and he did it.

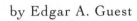

Notice the internal rhyme, meter, and rhythm in this poem—it's pure music! Below, I've typed the **stressed** syllables in CAPS so you can follow this pattern:

Example: SOMEbody SAID that it COULDn't be DONE,

But HE with a CHUckle rePLIED …

Do you hear the waltz-like rhythm in his lines? That's known as **meter**. Also, note how the last word in the first and third, and the second and fourth lines rhyme. That's called a **rhyme scheme**.

Traditional poetry is very structured and has strict rules for each form. The most common pattern of poetry is the **ballad**, which is written in meter and rhyme consisting of several four-lined stanzas (a stanza is the equivalent of a paragraph in writing). These poems are often set to music (hence, the name 'ballad'). See an example below:

A True Christian

by Ruth E. McDaniel

(1)	If you can smile and be at peace	(a)
(2)	and not respond in kind	(b)
(3)	when others are reviling you,	(c)
(4)	you have a Christian mind.	(b)

(5)	If you can feel compassion for	(d)
(6)	those who are set apart	(e)
(7)	because of illness, race, or creed	(f)
(8)	you have a Christian heart.	(e)
(9)	If you can give your life to God	(g)
(10)	regardless of the toll	(h)
(11)	then you can rest assured, my friend,	(i)
(12)	you have a Christian soul!	(h)

As you see, lines two and four, six and eight, ten and twelve, rhyme. So, the rhyme scheme in a **ballad** is identified as "a, b, c, b."

Each line of traditional poetry is measured according to its number of rhythmic beats (known as feet). A **foot** is the combination of groups of stressed and unstressed syllables that create a unique sound. The above poem has four feet (beats) in the first line and three feet in the second line; each line of poetry is referred to as a verse, and each line of verse is named:

Five Most Common Lines of Verse		
One foot	=	Monometer
Two feet	=	Dimeter
Three feet	=	Trimeter
Four feet	=	Tetrameter
Five feet	=	Pentameter

Using CAPS for the *stressed* portion of lines one and two, you can see the rhythm (feet):

Example: If YOU can SMILE and BE at PEACE = four feet (beats)

and NOT reSPOND in KIND, = three feet (beats)

The combinations of stressed and unstressed syllables in "feet" are also named:

Five Most Common Types of Feet		
Name	Examples	# of Syllables
iamb (iambic)	"if YOU can SMILE" =	1 unstressed, 1 stressed
anapest (anapestic)	"if you THINK that you CAN" =	2 unstressed, 1 stressed
trochee (trochaic)	"IF you TRY to" =	1 stressed, 1 unstressed
dactyl (dactylic)	"SOMEbody SAID that it" =	1 stressed, 2 unstressed
spondee (spondaic)	"NOW COMES" =	2 stressed

Using this information, we can identify the last poem as having three four-lined stanzas with an 'abcb' rhyme scheme. Additionally, the first line of verse is written in **iambic tetrameter** (1 unstressed, 1 stressed syllable; four feet).

When writing poetry, it's essential to use words that flow, words that fit the right rhythm—especially in traditional poetry. The stressed syllables should come naturally. For example, let's change the first line of verse from **iambic** to **trochaic** and see what happens:

Example: IF you CAN smile AND be AT peace …

It no longer sounds natural because we're stressing syllables that are normally unstressed.

Writing Exercise

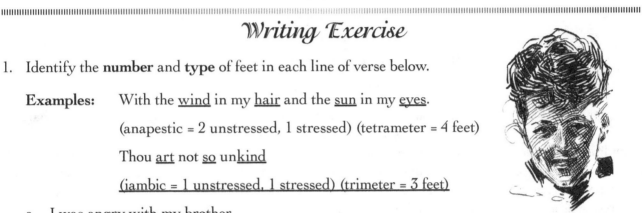

1. Identify the **number** and **type** of feet in each line of verse below.

    Examples: With the <u>wind</u> in my <u>hair</u> and the <u>sun</u> in my <u>eyes</u>.

    (anapestic = 2 unstressed, 1 stressed) (tetrameter = 4 feet)

    Thou <u>art</u> not <u>so</u> un<u>kind</u>

    <u>(iambic = 1 unstressed, 1 stressed) (trimeter = 3 feet)</u>

    a.   I was angry with my brother …

    _____

    b.   Merrily, merrily, will I sing …

    _____

    c.   When forty winters shall besiege thy brow …

    _____

2. Write the first stanza (four lines only) of a ballad using the 'abcb' rhyme scheme. The first and third lines of the verse should be written in iambic tetrameter (4 feet), and the second and fourth lines in iambic trimeter (3 feet).

    Example: I <u>wish</u> I <u>could</u> re<u>pay</u> you, <u>Lord</u>,

    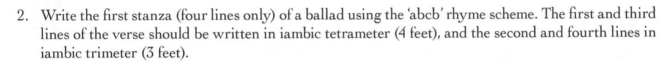

    for <u>all</u> that <u>You</u> have <u>done</u>.

    My <u>world</u> was <u>filled</u> with <u>storm</u> clouds; <u>You</u>

    re<u>placed</u> them <u>with</u> the <u>sun</u>.

Make sure your words flow smoothly and aren't stressed unnaturally. Do not force your rhyme: think of what you want to say, then find the words that fit. Your four-lined, rhymed message must make sense.

If you have trouble getting started, you may use one of the following as your first line of verse.

  1.   I thought I saw a blade of grass …

  2.   When Winter steps aside for Spring …

  3.   A feather floated through the air.

Your stanza: _____

_____

_____

_____

_____

Some contemporary poets consider traditional verse too old-fashioned, too sing-song-sounding (that's a good example of *alliteration* or *consonance*), and too restrictive. They prefer to write free verse—verse that doesn't follow a fixed pattern of meter, rhyme, or other conventional poetic rules.

A poet, however, must learn how to write traditional poetry before he can advance to free verse—just as an author must learn basic English skills (grammar and composition) before he can write a novel. Once you've mastered the art of writing structured poetry, you can experiment with unstructured form.

A group of French poets claim to have invented free verse during the late nineteenth century in order to eliminate the restrictions of formal metered poetry. (However, I already pointed out that portions of the Bible were written in free verse, so the French poets weren't the first; some biblical examples are located in the beginning of this chapter.) The French wanted to write unrhymed lines of different lengths and rhythms following the pattern of natural speech but maintaining emotional content and meaning.

Since then, free verse has flourished in the world of poetry and may even outnumber traditional verse today.

If I were to rewrite my poem in free verse form, it might look like this:

A True Christian

by Ruth E. McDaniel

Smile
be at peace.
Don't fear
verbal stones cast
but feel compassion
for all mankind.

Serve God
without conscious thought
of human cost.

Know
you have
a soul.

As you can see, the basic message is the same, but the two forms differ dramatically.

Writing Exercise

Rewrite your four-lined ballad on separate paper in free verse form, retaining the meaning or message but using fewer words. Remember, a free verse line doesn't follow conventional composition rules; most sentences are incomplete. Think of free verse as "poetic shorthand."

Prose

> PROSE *is a written form of language without rhythm or meter.*

It may be just as beautiful and imaginative as poetry, but in a different way. At times it is referred to as a *vignette* (pronounced "vin-yet"), which is a short literary sketch or description. In a broad sense, however, prose refers to almost any kind of writing other than poetry.

The following could be considered prose:

A Different View

by Ruth E. McDaniel

When I was a child, I spent two weeks every summer with my aunt and uncle who lived in Grafton, Illinois. Frequently, they took me to Pere Marquette State Park lodge which housed an eight-foot by eight-foot inlaid chess board on the floor of the great hall, with man-sized chessmen poised and waiting for the big game.

I was awestruck by those massive pieces!

Forty years later, I made plans to visit the lodge again. I excitedly told my neighbor about the gigantic chess board and players. Imagine my shock when those man-sized chessmen only came up to my waist now!

Writing Exercise

Using my example, write a short sketch (50 words will do) detailing your most recent vacation … a trip to the zoo … anything out-of-the-ordinary that happened to you. Don't try to use flowery language (remember, this isn't supposed to be poetic). Just write it down as you would tell it to a friend—and be sure to include your "senses" (sight, sound, touch, taste, smell), so we'll know exactly how you felt.

Fiction

> **FICTION is a written composition created from the imagination which not only tells a story but makes a statement about human character or experience.**

Fictitious literature is normally written in three forms: *novels, novelettes,* and *short stories.*

- ❦ *Novels* are narratives of more than 30,000 words. They're usually complex stories dealing with human experiences through sequential events (events that are listed in the order that they happened). Due to length, the characters, the setting, and the plot are developed in great detail.

- ❦ *Novelettes* are brief novels or long short stories usually ranging from 8,000 to 30,000 words. Plot and character development would not be as liberal as in novels.

- ❦ *Short stories* are compressed, effective stories of less than 8,000 words. The plot is developed and resolved in a single situation. Action must begin immediately, and the number of characters is limited. The writer must bring his story to a crisis and ultimate resolution using very few words. His theme should include a special moral awareness or a solid view of human experience. In spite of its brevity, the short story can be filled with meaning and significance.

In future chapters, we will focus on how to write fiction.

The Art of
Writing Creatively

Chapter Seven

Writing in the Light

Let the Word of Christ richly dwell within you with all wisdom, teaching and admonishing one another with psalms and hymns and spiritual songs, singing with thankfulness in your hearts to God. And whatever you do in word or deed, do all in the name of the Lord Jesus, giving thanks through Him to God the Father. —Colossians 3:16, 17

This passage, while speaking of music, may be applied to creative writing as well.

As you learn how to write creatively, you should consider how you might use it to glorify God. God has given you the gift of language and enables you to use it rightly. All of life and culture should be transformed by the power of the gospel, including your desire to write.

> *CREATIVE WRITING is using God's gift of language in a way that imitates His own creativity.*

First Things First

God created all things out of nothing. We, however, must create out of what already exists. No one ever writes something wholly new.

> Is there anything of which one might say, "See this, it is new"? Already it has existed for ages which were before us. There is no remembrance of earlier things; and also of the later things which will occur, there will be for them no remembrance among those who will come later still. —Ecclesiastes 1:10-11

Aim at creativity that is subject to the Lordship of Christ. Don't try to be totally original. Seek to tell the old, old story of Jesus and His love in a new and fresh way that captures the minds and hearts of your readers.

God's creative handiwork includes the Bible and its various literary forms. He is a poet, a maker of stories, and much more. God's example, which you should follow, is first among all forms of writing. The Bible therefore should be read as an inspiration for writing—but do not stop there. Let it also be the example for your own creativity. Great Christian writers such as John Bunyan, the writer of *Pilgrim's Progress*, and C. S. Lewis, the writer of the *Narnia Tales*, have employed God's Word as such an example.

The Greatest Story Ever Told

The key to writing a powerful work of literature is a deep understanding of the greatest story of the ages. It encompasses all the conflicts of history. It begins wonderfully yet tragically when God breathes life into man and man rebels against his Creator. Then it flows through the lives and history of the people of Israel, reaching its powerful climax in the drama of the cross. The story is carried forward in the life of the church as it comes into conflict with the kingdom of darkness, coming to a grand finale at the return of Christ.

Every effort to write creatively doesn't need to embrace all aspects of God's great story, but each should mirror key aspects of that drama. If you write a novel, poem, or article, your work should reflect the rich tapestry of God's written Word. God must be glorified in Christ by your words—whether they reveal the great truths of salvation and how they change lives, or explain the way biblical values triumph over the world's values, or expose the conflict between the children of darkness and the children of light, or describe the struggle that each child of God fights in this world. This is what distinguishes creative writing that is Christian.

Writing that is creatively Christian should arise from a heart that knows and loves the Lord. The believer's work will demonstrate a love for that which is pleasing in the sight of God.

The Master Storyteller

In the past, Christian literature was often too didactic and too "preachy," but not any longer. Christian authors have discovered what Jesus knew two thousand years ago—that you can often reach and teach more effectively by giving people interesting stories that have realistic themes, true-to-life situations, and practical but righteous resolutions, than by lecturing them.

Jesus used parables that people could relate to in order to teach spiritual truths. That is what Christian writers must do, as well—create stories in which ordinary people overcome modern-day problems through faith and by applying the teachings of God. Don't paint your characters all good or all bad (I don't know anyone like that, do you?), and don't resolve your stories in a way that is impossible for the reader to identify with. For example, if your central character is a juvenile delinquent who accepts Christ as his Savior, don't portray him as a saint thereafter; show the trials he faces and how he overcomes them. People are human, and they need to know that God will help them through their struggles. Remember how Peter denied Christ? I'd call that a major spiritual crisis. Yet, Peter's story gives ordinary people hope because he triumphed through Christ in spite of his sin. Infuse your characters with some personal shortcomings to make them lifelike; your readers will find their situations more believable.

Here's another example. In the following excerpt from one of my stories, Jeff, a sixteen-year-old high school student and a professed Christian, is facing a moral dilemma:

My Brother's Keeper[9]

"I'm trying to get dressed!"

"What's the matter? Don't you want to be 'friends'?"

---

9. Published by Christian Liberty Press.

Jeff looked back over his shoulder uneasily as his teammates surrounded Brian. Why didn't they leave him alone, Jeff wondered? Brian couldn't help it if he was born with a stunted arm.

"Hey, guys, you'd better put on your uniforms so we can start practice." Jeff tried to keep his voice low and unconcerned.

"We want Brian to show us his crippled arm," Bobbie replied viciously.

Jeff winced. "Well, I'll be out on the field. You'd better hurry up! You know how coach acts when you're late!" Jeff rushed past the group.

When he glanced back, he was relieved to see all four of them move away from Brian and walk toward their lockers. Brian looked sick. Jeff frowned and thought to himself, why didn't the poor kid tell somebody about the way the guys were harassing him? Mr. Winston, the principal, would change his schedule so he wouldn't have to be in the locker room when the football team arrived.

Jeff felt angry and guilty at the same time. He was becoming increasingly uncomfortable around his friends lately. They'd changed over the last couple of years. Jeff had known the four of them since starting Junior High. They used to have fun together, playing ball and camping. But, as they grew older, they started disagreeing over what constituted "fun."…

In this portion, I tried to show how Jeff was attempting to fit in with his friends, although he knew what they were doing was wrong. He turned his back on a fellow student and even felt angry with the innocent boy for putting him in that position. At the same time, he experienced a twinge of guilt. My character's going through the type of emotional upheaval that people can identify with.

In the following scene, it's the next day, and Jeff meant to talk with his friends about their behavior toward Brian, but the moment passed. Instead, he fosters the wild hope that the Christian values he lives by will somehow "rub off on them." However, as we all know, we are given many chances to learn our lessons in life. Once more, Jeff's friends are taunting Brian:

As Jeff approached, he was reminded of a program he had seen about African animal survival; his friends resembled a group of hyenas circling their prey! Suddenly, last Sunday's sermon came to mind: Am I my brother's keeper?

"All right, you guys, knock it off!" Jeff's voice was louder than he had intended.

Bobbie looked at Jeff in surprise. Then, his eyes narrowed and he said, "What's your problem? Is he a friend of yours?"

Eddie and Mark looked down at the ground, and Jason glanced toward the school.

"Not yet," Jeff responded. Brian watched him approach.

⟨⟩ ⟨⟩

As you can see, Jeff reached his decision—he would come to Brian's assistance even if it meant losing his friends. He faced the fact that, by doing nothing, he was actually condoning his friends' cruelty. Through this story, I was able to share with the reader the spiritual truth that maintaining your moral values outweighs every other consideration. Even though Jeff agonized over it, he finally decided he would rather be right with God than popular with his friends. It is much more effective to show the reader how a character deals with moral dilemmas than to tell him.

Truth Matters

Finally, brethren, whatever is *true*, whatever is *honorable*, whatever is *right*, whatever is *pure*, whatever is *lovely*, whatever is of *good repute*, if there is any *excellence* and if anything worthy of *praise*, dwell on these things. The things you have learned and received and heard and seen in me, practice these things; and the God of peace will be with you.—Philippians 4:8-9 (NASB)

Truth is a key criterion for writing. God is the God of truth, and His truth alone is enduring. Many novels have come and gone, but those that remain the most effective and virtuous embody God's truth. Good literature—whether factual or imaginary—tells the truth in love and has a deep honesty about it. It doesn't seek to create a new world out of one's own imagination but strives to portray reality as seen through the lens of God's Word.

Thus the Christian writer doesn't shrink from articulating the depraved aspects of man's sinful nature in his writing. Yet he won't glorify sin or indulge in a morbid fascination with the evil of the human heart. He writes in a fashion that is both biblical and balanced. For the believer, there is no glib romanticism, no idealistic fairy land, no endless sunny days. He is a realist who won't spin a web of tales that neglect the great conflict between light and darkness.

The Christian writer, though, is no pessimist—he never ends with the negative part of the story. Masterfully, he portrays the major theme of Christ's redemption. While men are dead in sin, Christ draws many to Himself and renews their lives for His glory. While some wicked characters will be portrayed as those who go from bad to worse, the story won't focus on them. It will center on those who fear God and do what is right in His eyes. They may be persecuted and cast down, but they won't be ridiculed forever. Instead, God's power will lead them to true and lasting victory.

After learning God's pattern of writing in Scripture, you should seek to learn from other Christians who have written well. Whether Augustine, Milton, Bunyan, C. S. Lewis, or Grace Irwin, compare their work with God's Word to see how they have built on His truth.

Let Your Light Shine

When I began to write professionally, I asked God to guide me in the direction He wanted me to go and to keep me on the right path (I still say this prayer daily). In addition, I asked Him to give me the ability to make my characters live on paper so they can bring His message to my readers.

I pray for all Christian writers to create courageously, to share God's Word in a way that makes readers want to know more. All Christians have received a commission from God—to spread His Word—to "Go into all the world and preach the good news to all creation" (Mark 16:15). "You are the light of the world … let your light shine before men.…" (Matthew 5:14, 16).

With the gift of writing comes a great responsibility. There is power in the written word. Let God lead the way and the words will flow, publishing doors will open, and hearts will hear His message through your writing.

I challenge you to *write in the light*! Let your words magnify the Lord!

Chapter Eight

What to Write About

As a writer, columnist, and conference speaker, I'm often asked, "What do you write about?" My first response is, "Everything!" But, that's not helpful to new writers. So, this chapter will detail where to find ideas and subjects worth writing about and how to develop them.

Read!

Reading the Bible, novels, poetry, newspapers, and magazines is a good place to start when searching for ideas. Some of my best material came after reading a phrase or a word that triggered a response in me.

For example, after reading a news article about a small boy who died of a brain tumor, I wrote a poem entitled "Paint a Rainbow in the Sky"—that was a phrase the child's mother used the day he died. That news story went straight to my heart, and I felt the need to write about it.

The 30-line traditional poem that resulted gives me a brief description of the boy's illness, his parent's faith, and the beautiful rainbow that formed following the child's death. My poem won a first place award, since then, and has been reprinted several times—so, it continues to touch people.

A magazine article about antiques made me wonder why people cherish and care for aged furniture but seem to reject elderly relatives. So, I wrote an essay entitled "Honored Antiques." It was published in a New York newspaper, December 1994. Hopefully, some writer will read my essay and be inspired to write one of his own. Ideas, concepts, and titles are not protected by copyright. So, feel free to experiment if something you read touches you.

Ask Questions

Why? What? Where? When? How? These questions are essential to every writer. And, of course, they're the foundation of good journalism. Question everything—then write down the answer.

Why does my nose start running when I'm exposed to cats? This would make a good article about allergies.

Why do little boys fight and little girls cry? Examine the emotional differences between males and females and write your findings.

What's in a name? Explore the impact of names and nicknames on lives.

Where can it be? I wrote and sold a humorous short fiction story called "The Case of the Missing Keys," based on a true event. Our cat had hidden my car keys in a secret niche in the kitchen, and the story revolves around their recovery.

Where? Try writing stories about your vacations.

How? 'How-to' articles are in great demand in all magazines. Are you a budding gardener, artist, musician? Write about your hobbies and interests, then share your writings with someone.

Look ... Listen ... Learn

Observe and make notes. Keep your eyes and ears open. Ask questions and take notes. Then, write about what you've seen and heard. I've written many stories about people I know. I've also used descriptions of real people in fictional situations.

In one story, two boys save a dog from a burning house. The story was fiction, but the heroes were based on two youngsters who live in my neighborhood.

In another short story, a boy finally learns how to ride his two-wheel bicycle when he tries to escape from a giant bumblebee. The bumblebee incident actually happened, but the boy already knew how to ride his bike. I just magnified and changed reality to liven up the story—that's the joy of writing fiction!

Picture your friends, relatives, and neighbors in a fictional story setting. Having real characters to work with, in the beginning, helps you to visualize them. Once you've trained yourself to describe your characters (size, weight, shape, habits, hair and eye color, etc.), you'll be able to create your own. But, remember, when using real characters, change names and identities to avoid controversy. We'll review character development in Chapter Ten.

Interviews

I write personal interviews, biographies, and short stories about interesting people. Senior citizens offer a wealth of information. Real stories of the horse and buggy days are as close as the nearest nursing home ... and they love company!

Interviewing people is easy. Ask the person you're interviewing if you can tape your conversation on a recorder. Take notes. Snap photos. Then, assemble your material and write an article or a short story about that person.

I've interviewed people from all walks of life. Last year, I wrote about a 90-year-old poet who was still actively writing and seeking publication. My article was published in a senior newspaper and reprinted in a writer's publication. Write down those memories before they disappear!

Dream

Did you ever wake up in the middle of the night having just dreamed the perfect story? Keep a pen and paper next to your bed and write down as much as you can remember. Chances are, the next morning it won't seem quite as brilliant—but, it's a start. I've written several poems and short stories in my sleep ... I was even able to salvage a few of them in the light of day.

Experiment

Try writing a short story about a biblical hero. The following is an excerpt from my short story entitled "Just a Dream." It's a fiction story based, in part, on the early life of King David and was published in 1994 by Christian Liberty Press.

Just a Dream

by Ruth E. McDaniel

"Move! Get out of the way, runt!"

David pulled over to the side of the road as three husky juniors raced past him. He sighed and started pedaling again. Being small for his age was a definite disadvantage! He was tired of being intimidated. His father assured him that he had experienced the same problems … until he was sixteen years old. That's when he grew 12 inches! If David followed the tradition of the males in his family, he should reach his proper height within the next year. Maybe he would be more confident then.

David sped up as the three boys disappeared around the corner. He was so intent on their progress that he didn't see the huge pothole just ahead of him, and he hit it full force! Before he knew what happened, David flew over the handlebars and landed on his head, instantly losing consciousness.

"What's this? Are you sleeping again?"

David slowly opened his eyes and tried to focus on the person standing over him.

The man prodded him again. "Awake! This is no time to take a nap. I have something for you to do!"

David rose painfully and rubbed the bump on his head. He looked around in confusion. "Where am I?"

"None of your nonsense, David. Arise! I want you to take these supplies to your brothers. They're with King Saul in Elah Valley. Now, off with you! Find out how they're getting along and bring me news of the battle!"

David stared at the old man in speechless wonder. He was dressed in strange, robe-like garments, and he held the reins of a goat and a heavy-laden donkey. Impatiently, the man shoved the reins into David's hands, who, when he looked down, saw that he was no longer wearing jeans and tennis shoes! Instead, he wore a knee-length tunic with a leather bag tied around his waist! Fearfully, David looked around. Not a street or a building was in sight; he was standing on a grassy hillside surrounded by sheep! What was happening?

"David! Enough dreaming! Your brothers are waiting!"

"Wh … where is Elah Valley?" the disoriented youth asked.

The old man snorted in disbelief. "Of all the sons of Jesse," he muttered to himself, "why the Lord chose David is beyond me!" Sternly, he looked down his formidable nose at the young man trembling before him. "Walk toward the sun! Now, begone before I forget that Samuel anointed you!" With that, the old man stomped away, grumbling under his breath.

David closed his eyes tightly and shook his head; his injury must be causing him to hallucinate. He slowly raised his eyelids and looked around again. No change. He was still standing on a hillside, holding the reins of a goat and a donkey!

David stared thoughtfully after the old man walking down the hill. Jesse?... Samuel? ... Anointed? His eyes suddenly opened wide! David! He was dreaming that he was David, from the Bible ... young David, before he defeated Goliath in Elah Valley!

He shook his head again, trying to clear his thoughts. Since he didn't know how this happened, or how to stop it, David had no choice but to "dream on." So, he tightened his grip on the reins and began walking toward the sun.

Any subject that interests you can be written in a variety of genres. Try your hand at writing poems, short stories, biographies, book reviews, and essays. Write a letter to the editor. Write a poem for a friend. Write a short story for a sibling. You will be surprised at how happy it makes people.

What should you write about? Everything—the sky's the limit!

Writing Exercise

Make a list of ten subjects you'd like to write a story about. Then, set your list aside—but, keep it handy. You will refer to that list soon.

Plot and Theme

> *A PLOT is a series of events and relationships forming the basis of a composition.*

> *A THEME is the subject or topic of a composition—an implied or stated insight about life or human nature.*

A *plot* is the plan or scheme of a literary story, whereas a *theme* is what the story is all about. "Plotting" is taking one of those subjects and developing a story out of it.

Once you've chosen your subject or theme, your next step will be to map out your plan. (We'll save the actual planning stage of the plot for Chapter Nine, "Making Your Outline.")

Did you know that there are only thirty-six basic plot situations available to all writers? Even back in Aristotle's time, it was reported that there were no new plots—they'd all been used! So, should you quit writing before you begin? No! Because what you do with your plot situation will make it new and different.

What are some of these plot situations?

- ❦ A mother searches for her son who ran away from home because of a misunderstanding: this is known as the "recovery of a lost loved one" plot.

- An ambitious man works hard for a promotion but his boss tries to block his progress: this is the "ambition" plot.

- A farmer appeals to a judge because the landlord is trying to take his property away from him: this is the "supplication" plot.

- A missionary gives his life to bring Christianity to pygmy tribes: this is the "self sacrifice for an ideal" plot.

- The king's brother tries to assassinate the king and seize the throne: this is the "rivalry of kinsmen" plot.

- An old woman is held hostage by a fugitive who eventually gives himself up to a caring hostage negotiator: this is the "falling prey to cruelty or misfortune" plot.

There are many others such as *revolt, abductor, deliverance, remorse, loss of loved ones, jealousy,* etc. Often, several of these plots are combined. For instance, a plot involving a "solicitor and adversary" blends well with "supplication" and "deliverance."

Writing Exercise

Did you see how I wrote out one-sentence explanations for the plot examples above? You should be able to state your plot situations in one sentence also.

Pull out the list of ten subjects that you'd like to write about (from the previous exercise) and rewrite them into ten one-sentence plot situations.

Examples:

Subject: <u>Daniel as a child.</u>

Plot Situation: <u>Daniel is carried off by King Nebuchadnezzar's army to Babylon where he struggles to remain faithful to the God of Israel.</u>

Subject: <u>Jim's grandmother is in a coma.</u>

Plot Situation: <u>Jim is determined to bring his grandmother out of her coma through constant communication, prayer, and love.</u>

1. Subject: _____

   Plot Situation: _____

   _____

2. Subject: _____

   Plot Situation: _____

   _____

3. Subject: _____

    Plot Situation: _____

    _____

4. Subject: _____

    Plot Situation: _____

    _____

5. Subject: _____

    Plot Situation: _____

    _____

6. Subject: _____

    Plot Situation: _____

    _____

7. Subject: _____

    Plot Situation: _____

    _____

8. Subject: _____

    Plot Situation: _____

    _____

9. Subject: _____

    Plot Situation: _____

    _____

10. Subject: _____

    Plot Situation: _____

    _____

Finding Your Voice

Every one of God's children is different. We look, act, and speak differently. That difference also carries into our writing—known as our "writing voice."

Think of three of your favorite authors. What do you like about their writing styles? Could you tell their work apart if you were given samples of each? If so, it's because you recognize their unique voices.

We're blessed by their differences. Can you imagine how dull reading would be if everyone wrote alike?

So, how do you find your unique writing voice?

Write! Write a lot! Write letters, descriptions, book reports, keep a journal—anything—but write every day.

- ❦ Do you like to write about people? about animals? about places? or, all of the above?
- ❦ Do you prefer to write about action-packed events or the quiet beauty of nature?
- ❦ Do you have more dialogue than description (narrative) in your compositions, or vice versa?

Maybe you don't know yet. If not, don't be concerned. As you progress through this textbook, you will begin to see a pattern emerge in your writing style. When you reach a point where your compositions sound as if you are speaking—you have found your writing voice. At that time, you will be comfortable with your writing, and the reader will be able to catch a glimpse of your personality through your work.

However, it does not happen overnight. Just as professional ice skaters practice for years to achieve a smooth performance, you must study, write, study, and write some more. It takes time for your writing to sound natural and be grammatically correct as well. And, you will continue to improve throughout your life.

Chapter Nine

Making Your Outline

So far, you have sharpened your grammar and composition skills, studied complete sentences and complete paragraphs, learned where to get ideas for your writing, and studied plot. Then you chose ten subjects you would like to write about and reworked them into ten one-sentence plot situations.

Now we are ready to discuss outlines. An outline is a sketch, draft, or skeleton of a subject, speech, or written work. For example, the following could be considered an outline of creative writing because it summarizes the most important points:

Creative Writing From A to Z

A **Action.** Use lots of action verbs (and fewer weak adjectives) to keep your readers interested.

B **Believable.** Make sure your characters, events, and settings sound realistic and lifelike.

C **Conflict and Climax.** In a good fiction story, your main character must face a conflict that grows until it reaches a climax; he then resolves the problem or learns from it.

D **Dialogue and Description.** Use plenty of dialogue to keep your story moving smoothly; write complete and detailed descriptions so your reader can "see" the scenes.

E **Editing and Ending.** Edit, rewrite, and polish your work until it's as good as you can make it; always give your readers a satisfactory ending.

F **Fresh.** Use fresh, original similes, metaphors, and comparisons—don't tarnish your work by using worn-out expressions (clichés).

G **Goal.** Set practical goals for yourself: decide to write a chapter a day, or 1,000 words (four pages) a day, or whatever you think you can handle.

H **Humor.** Add a touch of humor to even your serious compositions.

I **Inspiration.** Try to write on a worthy theme that will inspire your readers; let God inspire, illuminate, and enlighten you so you can enlighten others, in turn.

J **Just.** Let your stories be well-grounded in biblical truth, conscientious, fair, unbiased and equitable.

K **K.I.S.S.** "Keep It Short and Simple"; keep your narrative and dialogue understandable; don't try to impress readers with profound language (don't use 50¢ words where 5¢ words will do); use short sentences rather than long, rambling ones.

L **Love and Logic.** Let the love of God shine through your words; advance your story plot and characters in logical, reasonable steps.

M **Mood.** Set the mood of your story by using sensory details (sight, sound, smell, taste, touch) and vivid descriptions to involve the reader emotionally.

N **Name and Nouns.** Choose appropriate names for your characters (according to their ages and time frame); use concrete nouns in place of weak adjectives.

O **Outline.** Preparing outlines, even for short stories, will help you arrange your ideas to give you direction and guidance. It will make writing the story much easier.

P **Plot.** A solid plot is the combination of a well-developed central character, secondary characters, a major conflict, an attempt to resolve it, the final resolution, and how it changed your main character.

Q **Question.** Answer the questions: who? what? where? when? why? and how? in order to write the most complete story possible.

R **Rewrite.** The least enjoyable but most important part of writing is rewriting.

S **"Show, Don't Tell."** Use dialogue and narrative to show the reader what's happening—don't tell the reader. (The one exception is in writing outlines; then, you "tell, don't show" for brevity's sake.)

T **Tension.** As you write, allow the tension to build until you reach the turning point (climax) of your story—this will keep your reader involved and interested.

U **Unite.** Combine the varied parts of your story into one harmonious whole; don't leave any loose ends.

V **Variety and Voice.** Vary the length of sentences, the types and locations of speaker IDs, the settings, and characters; find your writing "voice"—your unique writing style.

W **Write and Worthy.** Write! Write! Write! "Practice makes perfect"—the more you write, the better you will write. And choose a worthy theme or subject—make sure your story is worth telling about.

X **"X-out."** Delete any portion of your composition that interrupts the smooth flow of, or isn't pertinent to, your story. If it's a clever phrase or a "gem" that you don't want to lose, save it for another story.

Y **Yield** up your pen to the Lord—write to bring Him glory. He blesses those who are committed to using their writing talents to further His Kingdom.

Z **Zeal.** Be passionate, eager, ardent, and enthusiastic about your writing—it will show in your work.

Arrange Your Ideas

The purpose of an outline is to map out your story to give you direction and guidance. Arranging your ideas in outline form will also help you find a clear and logical order of presentation. Few writers are talented enough to create complete stories in logical order and with all the correct details without written outlines to guide them.

Outlines should:

- be written in third person (he, she, it, they).

- be written in present tense.

- have a beginning, a middle, and an end:

  - **Beginning.** To give your story character and direction, introduce a *central character* who is interesting, lifelike, and motivated—someone the reader cares about. Set the *mood*. Establish *conflict* which is essential to your story; the main character must try to overcome this problem or learn a lesson from it.

  - **Middle.** Bring in *secondary characters* who are key people in the main character's life, advance the *plot* by developing your story naturally, and worsen the conflict by putting obstacles in the way.

  - **End.** Reach a climax, or turning point, in your story and end it with a final resolution which satisfies the reader.

As examples, I'll use two of my own situations (one-sentence story summaries) and show how I developed them into outlines.

Outline One

Working Title: <u>The King's Quest</u>

Plot Situation: <u>A king discovers his trusted aides have duped him and abused his people; he resolves to correct this wrong.</u>

First, I wrote a short summary of the entire story. As I wrote the summary, I sectioned off the beginning, the middle, and the end.

Note: In a summary, you need only give the facts—so, in this case, "tell, don't show."

Beginning

King John has a dream in which a village boy informs him that his people are poor, hungry, and over-taxed by the king's ministers. The king had allowed his father's advisors to take over his duties after his father died because he was young and inexperienced and unsure of how to rule a kingdom.

When the king awakes, he wonders if the accusations are true. To find out, he formulates a plan.

Middle

A beggar is seen on the palace grounds asking for food and shelter. The king's ministers are incensed and call out the guards, the hunting dogs, and all the servants to find him.

The beggar escapes to the nearest village where he receives assistance from a young widow and her daughter. Although the widow is poor and has little food, she shares what she has with the beggar (who calls himself Alfred).

Alfred meets several of the villagers who welcome him and give him food, shelter, and a job. He questions them about their lives and their relationships to the king.

End

The king's messenger rides through the countryside announcing that someone has kidnapped the king, and the royal army is searching for them everywhere. Shortly, the king's soldiers arrive and confront the villagers. At this point, Alfred washes the ashes from his face and hair, stands up straight, and declares that the beggar and the king are one and the same.

King John returns to the palace and assembles his people. Dressed in his royal robes and crown, the king tells the assembly about his dream and his quest for the truth. He accuses the ministers of multiple misdeeds and banishes them from the kingdom for all time.

Then, King John introduces his newfound friends and tells of their charity and kindliness toward him. He proclaims a new regime of reasonable laws and minimal taxes, and bestows offices and titles on several of the villagers.

The king's news is received with gratitude and thanksgiving, and the kingdom looks forward to a brighter and more blessed future.

List of Characters

Now that I had a general outline, I decided to put together a list of characters:

Primary Character: *King John/Alfred*, the beggar

Secondary Characters: Minister of Justice: rules over courts

Minister of Finances: controls taxes, income, and the king's Treasure Room

Minister of Provisions: oversees food supplies and staples

Minister of Royal Guards: heads the king's army

Minister of Transportation

Minister of Education

Minister of Housekeeping

Minister of the Arts

King's messenger

Mary: the village washerwoman

Rachel: Mary's daughter

Father Roland: the village carpenter and pastor

Mother Abigail: Father Roland's wife

Tom, Bartholomew, Joshua: Father Roland's sons

Esther: Father Roland's daughter

Big George: the village blacksmith

Bess: Big George's daughter

Jacob: Big George's son

Note: As I wrote the story, I changed the outline or list of characters as needed. A story will often develop a life of its own— when this happens, and if the new direction seems to work even better, be flexible and allow for the changes.

After completing the outline and list of characters, I was ready to name my chapters:

Working Title: The King's Quest (goal: a 10,000 word mini-novel)

Beginning: Chapter 1—King John has dream

Middle: Chapter 2—Beggar invades palace

Chapter 3—Beggar escapes to village; meets Mary

Chapter 4—Alfred meets Father Roland

Chapter 5—Big George hires Alfred

End: Chapter 6—Messenger announces king's kidnapping

Chapter 7—King discloses his identity

Chapter 8—King calls for general assembly, dismisses his evil ministers, and appoints the good villagers

The next step was to "flesh out" my characters (we will work on character development in Chapter Ten).

Finally, it was time to write the story. By constantly checking my character list, descriptions, and outline as I wrote, I seldom strayed from the plot, and I was able to stay focused—it truly was a map that led me step by step from beginning to end!

After I began writing the story, I tried to finish at least one full chapter at a sitting so I wouldn't lose my train of thought or change the flow or mood. The end result was a marketable 10,000-word mini-novel.

Outline Two

Working Title: <u>Learning To Trust</u> (goal: a 7,000 word mini-novel)

Plot Situation: <u>Through a tragic accident, Becky becomes a paraplegic at the age of fifteen and must learn to put her trust in God.</u>

. . . .

Beginning

Becky's wheelchair plunges over the side of a hiking trail and ends up at the bottom of a ravine. Becky is shaken and doesn't know if she's hurt, so she sends her support dog, Buck, for help. While she's waiting, she thinks back to her accident one year earlier (this is known as a "flashback") when she rode her bike into the path of an oncoming car. The collision caused Becky irreversible spinal damage.

. . . .

Middle

Facing a lifetime in a wheelchair, Becky sinks into a deep depression. Her family, friends, and church pastor pray with her and for her. When she reaches her lowest point, Becky finally turns to God for help. For the first time in her life, she must learn to put her total trust in the Lord and live moment by moment.

. . . .

End

Becky gets a support dog to improve her mobility and independence but discovers she's unable to return to her original school. That's when she hears about home schooling. This turns out to be a blessing for Becky (and for her little brother). Now, it's a year later. As she calmly waits for the help to arrive, she realizes how far she has come in trusting the Lord and in adjusting to her physical challenge. In fact, she's able to calm her mother and direct her own rescue.

List of Characters

Primary Character: *Becky Rogers*

Secondary Characters: *Stephen and Deborah Rogers*: Becky's parents

Ryan Rogers: Becky's little brother

Mr. & Mrs. Rogers: paternal grandparents

Mr. & Mrs. Lewis: maternal grandparents

Pastor Richards

Dr. Gonzales: Pediatric Neurosurgeon

Miscellaneous nurses and therapists

Nancy: a paraplegic sent to tell Becky about Support Dogs, Inc.

Baron: Nancy's support dog

Donna: Support Dog staff person

Buck: Becky's support dog

Mr. & Mrs. Brown and son *Peter*: Christian home school support group

Since this story runs less than 10,000 words, it wasn't necessary to name chapters. So, I "fleshed out" my characters, gathered my research material on Support Dogs and Christian home schooling—and began to write.

Writing Exercise

1. Choose one of your ten plot situations from Chapter Eight and write a general outline using my outlines as examples. Remember to tell the facts only and section off (a) the beginning, (b) the middle, and (c) the end. This writing exercise should be done on separate paper.

2. Prepare a list of characters based on your general outline. Then, set them aside; we'll "flesh them out" in the next chapter.

Chapter Ten

Developing Your Characters

$\mathcal{A}$re you getting excited yet? You should be! You are coming to the fun part—it's time to create life-like characters.

You have chosen a subject, written a plot situation, developed an outline, and listed your cast of characters. Now, you must "flesh out" your characters to make them live and breathe on the page. Since you have given your primary character a name (we will address name selection in great detail in Chapter Eleven), you probably already have a vague impression of what he/she looks like. Is he real to you yet? If your character seems stiff and unbelievable to you, then he won't be real to your readers either.

Characterization comes naturally to some writers, while others seem to struggle with it. Let's review how to make your characters believable—people your readers can visualize and care about.

Seven Steps to Characterization

1. Give a complete description of the person's physical appearance.

I told you earlier that you can use a real live person as a model—but be sure to change some features so he won't recognize himself on the page. What are the unique physical traits that make this person different? Don't describe him as "tall, dark, and handsome." Be specific:

He's eighteen years old	a slim, athletic build
5' 11" tall	a prominent nose—slightly crooked (broken years before)
weighs 160 pounds	alternates contact lenses with wire-framed glasses
has short, dark, wavy brown hair	several pock marks on face (chicken pox when he was ten)
heavy, dark eyebrows, brown eyes	has a springy walk, likes to run upstairs
a ruddy complexion	swings arms vigorously when he walks

Are you beginning to picture this person? The more specific you are, the more lifelike your character will become.

Frequently, as I flip through the weekend newspaper ads, I will see a model who fits the vague image of one of my characters. I cut out the picture of the model, tape it to a piece of paper, write my character's name at the top of the page, and fill in the missing details—a specific description of that person, using this list as a guide.

2. Describe his voice.

Is his voice strong and deep, or thin and weak? Does he speak smoothly or does he mumble or stutter? Does he talk high or low, loud or soft, fast or slow?

Voices are very distinctive—you can usually recognize a caller's voice on the telephone before he identifies himself. What part of the country is he from? Midwesterners have one type of accent (said to be nasal), while people from the East talk fast, people from the South may have a drawl, etc.[10]

Have you noticed that you can tell if a person is smiling or frowning from the tone of his voice? By use of vivid description, the reader will be able to 'hear' your character.

3. List his good and bad qualities.

One mistake new writers often make is in painting a picture of a person who is all good or all bad. I've never met anyone like that—I doubt if they exist. People are human. Be truthful and let your readers see the weak side of your "good" character and some positive side of your "bad" character. Perhaps the hero is a "good Christian," but tends to be too impatient with indecisive people. And, maybe the "villain" loves his mother. By adding these human qualities, your character becomes more real and fully rounded.

4. Describe his personality.

Is he shy or confident, affectionate or cool and distant? Does he smile a lot? Is he quick to laugh? Is he negative or positive, logical or whimsical, volatile or easygoing? Your character can even be both—he can start out by being negative and distrustful, and end up becoming loving and kind; however, the transition must be a natural one to be believable. Few people have the kind of experience that Saul had on the road to Damascus (Acts 9). Each person is an individual—even fictional characters. Be sure to give him qualities that ring true; a person of strong faith should be able to withstand peer pressure. If not, why not? Use your imagination—become your character—try to put yourself in his place and write down your impressions. Don't leave out any details. This will not only help your readers identify with your character, but it will help you understand how your primary and secondary characters interact and relate to each other.

5. Describe his dress style.

Does your character dress neatly, or does he wear whatever's handy? Is he dressed in the latest fashion or in hand-me-downs? Are his clothes pressed and clean, or torn and dirty? Does he mix stripes with checks or coordinate his clothing well? Is he a student or fully employed? Does he wear penny loafers and argyle socks, or worn sneakers and tube socks?

Does his clothing match his personality? A person's lifestyle and identity are usually reflected in his wearing apparel. Be consistent—don't describe your subject as quiet, studious, and mild mannered,

---

10. Don't try to write dialect, but write the words that regional people use.

but wearing gaudy clothing and a mohawk haircut! Your readers will not be able to reconcile the two images—unless you are writing about a very confused character.

6. *Describe his hobbies, habits, and peculiarities.*

Is he the athletic type who plays basketball every chance he gets, or does he prefer to sit at his computer hour after hour? Does he collect baseball cards, postage stamps, snakes, old records? Does he have a nervous tic (clearing his throat, fidgeting, blinking constantly)? Does he have good study habits or rarely complete assignments? Is he always on time or usually tardy? Does he prefer health food or junk food? Does he reject authority or follow rules?

7. *Describe his life-attitude, relations to others, and general outlook.*

Is your character someone who respects himself and others, or is he lacking in self-regard? Is he motivated and ambitious? Is he a good brother, son, cousin, student, worker? Why? If not, why not? Does he have a positive outlook on life, or is he unsure and afraid? What are his overall feelings, emotions, and attitudes? How does he react to people—and how do they react to him?

Following all of these steps may seem like a waste of time, but it will make your fictional characters come to life. The longer the story, the more important it is for you to really get to know your primary and secondary personas. Don't worry if the listed features seem repetitive; "qualities," "personality," and "life-attitude" often share the same traits. The idea is to create an individual who is unique and comes alive on the page. The more features you list, the more real your creation will seem to you—and to your readers.

Writing Exercise One

In the last chapter, you wrote the general outline of a story and made a list of characters. From that list, write on separate paper a profile of your principal character using all seven characterization steps.

The following example is the profile (called a "character sketch") of a make-believe person I created for one of my stories:

WORKING TITLE: *The New Neighbor*

by Ruth E. McDaniel

PRIMARY CHARACTER SKETCH:

Name: Luke Trotter

1. *Physical Appearance*
5'9" tall

47 years old but looks older

weighs 172 pounds, slightly overweight

average facial features, square chin

heavy eyebrows, wrinkles around eyes and mouth

Salt-and-pepper hair, crew cut, clean-shaven

light blue eyes, pale skin, (stays out of the sun)

walks slowly, uses a cane, often staggers

(has multiple sclerosis but tries to hide it)

2. Voice

deep and pleasant

speaks slowly and distinctly

has slight Southern accent

slurs words when overly tired

3. Good/bad qualities

abrupt with people when feeling weak

studious, loves to read

dislikes noise and domestic animals

his pride won't allow him to accept help from others

enjoys talking to children

kind to the elderly

intellectual, supports the arts

obeys the law, conscientious voter

strong Christian beliefs

took care of his mother until she died

4. Personality

can be moody, impatient

quiet, courteous

warm smile, rare infectious laugh

gives impression of self-assurance

happy around children, especially his nieces and nephews

generous and thoughtful

loves flowers and classical music

can't tolerate heat and high humidity

writes stories for children under pseudonym

5. Dress Style

wears lightweight, loose clothing

clothes are worn but clean and neat

sandals and white cotton socks

long-sleeved shirts; tan, gray, blue colors

khaki trousers

hats and dark sunglasses to shade eyes/face from sun

dresses appropriately for formal occasions

6. Hobbies, habits, peculiarities

plays piano, mostly classical music

works at freelance writing, Mon.–Fri., from 9:00 a.m. to 4:00 p.m.

collects animal figurines

punctual, can't abide tardiness

smells food before eating it

whistles when nervous

likes to sit on the dark front porch late at night and rock

reads the Bible for one hour each day

drums his fingers on his knees when thinking

7. Life-Attitude, relation to others, general outlook

good life-attitude but a loner

motivated to provide good Christian reading material to children

no ambition to become famous author

self-conscious about his chronic illness

loves the Lord; doesn't fear death

uneasy around strangers

general outlook fluctuates according to his physical status

very close to his siblings and their children

never married

relates best to children and the elderly

Does it sound like I'm describing a real person? Good! That was my goal. As you write your story, you'll want to refer frequently to your character's sketch so his personality, habits, peculiarities, and dress style are consistent.

Writing Exercise Two

Start a "Character Sketchbook." Using a notebook or journal, write physical descriptions and personal characteristics of six people you know, including interesting people you've seen in person, in a movie, or on television. Describe their profiles, what they wear, how they speak, scars or other identifying features—both pleasant and unpleasant. Do they have nervous tics (blinking, fidgeting, etc.)? Describe them. Do they walk with a smooth gait or in a disjointed, jerky fashion? How do these people affect you? Write down your reaction—that's probably how they will affect your secondary characters, as well. Update this journal regularly. It will give you a head start on future profiles.

Begin this writing project by writing your first character sketch in the space below.

1. Physical Appearance:

_____

_____

_____

_____

2. Voice:

_____

_____

_____

_____

3. Good/Bad Qualities:

_____

_____

_____

_____

4. Personality:

_____

_____

_____

_____

5. *Dress Style:*

_____

_____

_____

_____

6. *Hobbies, habits, peculiarities:*

_____

_____

_____

_____

7. *Life-Attitude, relation to others, general outlook:*

_____

_____

_____

_____

Chapter Eleven

What's in a Name?

How necessary are names? Well, just think of the chaos there would be in a world without names. How would we refer to a person, place, or thing? How would we communicate with them or distinguish between them?

God in His wisdom gave us many names. For example, I am known as a woman, wife, mother, grandmother, sister, daughter, aunt, cousin, friend, neighbor, American citizen, Christian, poet, writer, Ruth Eleanor McDaniel, and so on.[11]

> *A NAME is the word or combination of words by which a person, place, or thing can be identified or distinguished.*

Choosing the Right Name

"The year is 1995 and three-year-old Mable Thorton is chasing soap bubbles in her back yard."

What's wrong with this?

Answer: the little girl's name.

Do you know any three-year-olds named Mable? I'd be astonished if you did. Mable was a popular name long ago, but it's rare to find a baby named Mable in the 1990s. Nor will you find children named Alphaeus, Agrippa, or Cleopatra.

You will want to make your story as realistic as possible, and that includes naming your characters appropriately.

---

11. Although, when I was a child, I thought my name was Doris-Marie-Ruthie … that's what my mother would call me when she was excited about something. She would run through the names of my older sisters until she came to mine. I found myself doing the same thing when my three sons were growing up.

Finding the Right Name

How do you find names appropriate for your characters' ages? The same way I do.

- List the names and ages of all your friends and relatives.

- For the ages of newborn to five years, I clip the birth announcements from the newspapers. You can also buy a baby name book, but the birth announcement column has always provided me with more names than I ever needed, so save your money.

- For the six through eighteen-year-olds, I read the local journal newspapers on school events. You can borrow a young neighbor's school yearbook, too.

- The nineteen through forty-nine age group can also be found in the birth announcement column—they're the parents of the newborns.

- The final group, those in their fifties and above, can be found in the obituary columns; the dates of birth are given, as well as the survivors (an additional source of names and ages).

Then, of course, every writer owns a nearly endless list of first and last names—the telephone book.

Don't ruin your story by naming your characters inappropriately. Using proper names for the proper age groups gives your story the necessary realism.

Writing Exercise

Fill in ten (first and last) names each for the following age groups using the sources listed above.

0–5 yrs	First Names	Last Names
1.		
2.		
3.		
4.		
5.		
6.		
7.		
8.		
9.		
10.		

6–18 yrs	First Names	Last Names
1.		
2.		
3.		
4.		
5.		
6.		
7.		
8.		
9.		
10.		

19–49 yrs	First Names	Last Names
1.		
2.		
3.		
4.		
5.		
6.		
7.		
8.		
9.		
10.		

50+ yrs	First Names	Last Names
1.		
2.		
3.		
4.		
5.		
6.		
7.		
8.		
9.		
10.		

Choosing the Right Title

We have established that names are essential. But what about titles for stories, poems, or articles? How important is it to have a title?

Once again, it's a matter of convenience. It's much easier to identify or differentiate between written works with this needed label.

Not only are titles important to identify a written work, but the right title can actually attract people and make them want to read your story. For instance, which story would you rather read:

Dull: "The Early Days of Radio" (or)

Bright: "Don't Touch That Dial!"

I think it's safe to say the second title would draw more readers than the first.

A title should tie in with the theme of your story and arouse the reader's interest at the same time. Let's review some interesting and successful (in other words, published) titles.

Interesting Titles	Authors
Who Ever Heard of Farkleberry?	T. Weber
Are There Any More Out There Like Me?	L. Murphy
Graham Crackers, Galoshes, and God	B. Snyder
Trixie and the Tootlebug	R. McDaniel
The Midnight Intruder	G. Roper
Lobo, the King of Currumpaw	E. Thompson
Rikki-Tikki-Tavi	R. Kipling
Good Morning, Miss Dove	Patton
Annie and the Ogglewomp	R. McDaniel
Sam Weller Makes His Bow	C. Dickens
The Grave Grass Quivers	Kantor
The Strange Ride of Morrowbie Jukes	R. Kipling
Whoa, Car!	R. McDaniel
The Lake of the Dismal Swamp	T. Moore
Blessed Are the Peacemakers	C. Spurgeon
It Could Be Worse!	R. McDaniel
Beethoven and the Blind Girl	J. Todd
Samuel Spickelmeier and the Saratoga City Spelunkers	S. Kramer
Behold the Face of My Father	R. McDaniel
Where There's a Will There's a Way	E. Cook
Drop a Pebble in the Water	J. Foley
The Rose Still Grows Beyond the Wall	A. Frink
The Land of Beginning Again	L. Fletcher
The Breath of Life	R. McDaniel

Interesting Titles	Authors
The Town of Don't-You-Worry	I. Bartlett
Out Where the West Begins	A. Chapman
Just a Dream	R. McDaniel
The African Chief	W. Bryant
Is it True?	S. Williams
The Hidden Line	J. Alexander
The Kneeling Camel	A. Whitney
The Search for the City of Satisfaction	R. McDaniel
Old Yeller	F. Gipson

Writing Exercise

Create in the space below a list of ten original, intriguing titles. They can be based on outlines of stories you have already written, or for stories you hope to write in the near future. Hold onto these titles; they could stimulate, motivate, and inspire you. I've been known to write an entire story around a title—that's how important a good title can be!

1. _____

2. _____

3. _____

4. _____

5. _____

6. _____

7. _____

8. _____

9. _____

10. _____

Chapter Twelve

Begin with a Punch!

We've already discussed plot, developing realistic characters, and choosing appropriate names. In this chapter, we'll discuss effective use of strong beginning sentences to "hook" or "grab" your readers and make them want to continue reading your story.

"Grabbers"

Your opening sentence can make or break your story. Whether you're writing fiction or nonfiction, if you don't win the reader's interest in the very beginning, you'll lose him.

Today's readers are busier than ever. If they decide to take time out to read your work, it must grab and hold their attention. Don't bore them with minor details or excessive descriptions. Immediately bring them into the story; you can always "flash back" and fill them in on necessary facts as the story develops.

Well-known authors have discovered a secret—a good writer begins the story with action, dialogue (conversation), a question, a strong statement, or conflict. This is especially important when writing short stories.

By way of example, let's review the following introductory sentences (taken from my short stories and devotionals) and identify the different types of openings:

Story Title	Introductory Sentence	Opens with...
"Flight Plan"	Ruth popped her ears to equalize the pressure in them as soon as the plane leveled off.	an action
"What a Coincidence!"	"I can't believe my eyes," Ken said in amazement.	a dialogue
"When the Weather Outside is Frightful …"	It's hard to feel happy when it's only two degrees outside!	a statement
"Boring Bonnie"	"Hurry up, Bonnie! We're going to be late!" Cindy tapped her foot and glared at her wristwatch.	a dialogue
"Breaking the Code"	The Bible-study youth group buzzed with excitement.	an action
"Radical"	"You must be kidding!" Nathan cried.	a dialogue
"The Hair-Raising"	Jason stared in horror at the clumps of curly blond hair clinging to his comb.	an action

Story Title	Introductory Sentence	Opens with...
"Bankrupt"	"I've never felt so humiliated," Becky muttered.	a dialogue
"The Prevaricator"	"I lied … I'm … very sorry."	a dialogue
"The Coma"	Jim pulled a chair next to his grandmother's hospital bed, picked up her lifeless hand, and began to speak.	an action
"A Good Deed Resolution"	"Mom, I emptied the waste can and set the trash out by the curb."	a dialogue
"Learning to Trust"	"Go for help, Buck! Get Mother!"	a dialogue

Dialogue

You probably already noticed that I like to start my stories with a **dialogue**. Of the twelve opening sentences listed above, I used dialogue seven times, I used action four times, and I only used a statement once.

How do you decide which type of opening sentence to use? That depends on your story.

In "Flight Plan," the central character (a grandmother named Ruth) is flying to a speaking engagement. The young man who occupies the seat next to her is obviously nervous about flying, so she tries to distract him through conversation. During the course of that conversation, Ruth is able to witness to him.

Since this story is only 750 words long, I had to delete all excess details. I begin my story with Ruth 'popping' her ears after takeoff. As the story develops, we learn that Ruth has white hair and wears bifocals. That shows the reader she's elderly without our having to say it; not only does this save valuable words, but it also follows the "show, don't tell" rule.

You might ask—why did I open the story with Ruth "popping" her ears? The answer is, it was more interesting than saying, "Ruth unfastened her seat belt." Your goal is to get your reader involved in the story as quickly as possible. One way to accomplish that is to tell them something they can relate to (such as popping your ears after takeoff to equalize the air pressure).

Other opening sentences might have worked just as well:

- "Is this your first flight?" Ruth asked the young man sitting next to her.
- Ruth caught sight of the foot jiggling nervously next to her own.
- "My son used to shake his foot just like that whenever he was nervous," Ruth commented to the young man seated beside her.

As the author, you have total control over your story. You can start it any way you feel will cause your reader to want to turn the page.

In "Bankrupt," I used the central character's statement ("I've never felt so humiliated,") to hook my readers. Teenage Becky watches her parents sell their personal belongings at a garage sale. Her father's computer business failed, and her parents had to declare bankruptcy.

I put myself in Becky's place: how would I feel if I was a teenager facing her situation? It's normal for a young person to be embarrassed in a position like this—afraid your friends will find out your predicament. Thankfully, her father reminded her that God was in control of their lives and would guide them in the right direction.

Writing Exercise

1. Write three alternative opening sentences for "Bankrupt!" How would you begin this story? Pick up your pen and experiment. What device would you use to win a reader's interest: *action? dialogue? question?* How would you react if you were Becky?

Note: Do not forget to use *onomatopoeias* (words that imitate sounds), *exclamation points*, *similes*, etc. Use several writing tools to spice up your introductory sentence.

---

a. _____

_____

b. _____

_____

c. _____

_____

2. After reading the following story outlines, write one opening sentence for each. Make it a "grabber."

a. Your central character, Scott, faces a dilemma—either help his best friend, Jason, cheat on his math exam, or lose his friendship.

_____

_____

b. While baby-sitting, Sharon (your central character) thinks the toddler swallowed some pills. Does she dial #911 or call her mother?

_____

_____

c. Meagan was having a good time at Sarah's birthday party until she saw another friend, Angie, take a small present off the table and slip it into her pocket! Should she confront Angie? Should she tell Sarah?

_____

_____

Chapter Thirteen

Describe in Detail

Storytelling is one of the oldest forms of entertainment. People who are skilled in storytelling use body language, hand gestures, facial expressions, and different tones of voice to capture their audiences. They are narrating their stories.

Writers, however, don't have the advantage of personal contact with their readers. They have to rely on their expert use of words to make a story come alive. When you think of your favorite authors, you know it's possible. We have all read novels that were hard to put down. That's because we were gripped by the author's imagination and skillful use of narrative, details, dialogue, plot, etc.

Successful fiction writers have learned the five basic elements of good stories:

- ❦ Strong beginning
- ❦ Vivid description and dialogue
- ❦ Solid plot development
- ❦ Forceful climax
- ❦ Satisfactory ending

In this chapter, we'll work on vivid description and necessary details.

How do you describe in detail?

A writer must be more observant than the average person. For instance, when a writer looks at a painting, he needs to take note of his feelings (what he felt when he first saw the painting) and the subject matter. He needs to collect information about the artist. When was the painting finished? Where? What materials were used (is it an oil painting on canvas)? He must note the method used, the color scheme, the frame, etc. No detail is too minor for a writer; he knows that it's better to collect too much information than too little.

When describing a setting, try to give as complete a description as possible (depending on word limits, of course). In order to make the reader "see" what you (the writer) are describing, make it as realistic as possible. For example, when describing a dress—what color is it? What style? What design, or material? Is it new or old, bright and crisp or faded and torn?

Use your five senses when writing descriptions: sight, sound, smell, taste, and touch. Are there trees in the scene? What kind (oak, cherry, elm)? What kind of grass, weeds, or flowers? Is it a forest or an open field? Are there animals, birds, or insects? Are there lakes or ponds? What does the sky look like—is it clear and blue, or are dark clouds building, threatening? What does it smell like? What is the temperature like? Are there any cabins, houses, or other structures nearby? What do they look like?

Unless your reader can "see what you're seeing," he won't be able to follow your story. If you can't paint a vivid word picture of a frightening scene, for example, the reader will wonder why your character is so afraid—he won't become involved in the plot and he'll quickly lose interest and stop reading.

To demonstrate how important it is to give a complete description, look what happens when people are left to reach their own conclusions:

The Blind Men and the Elephant

by John Godfrey Saxe (1816–1887)

It was six men of Indostan
    To learning much inclined,
Who went to see the elephant
    (Though all of them were blind),
That each by observation
    Might satisfy his mind.

The First approached the elephant,
    And, happening to fall
Against his broad and sturdy side,
    At once began to bawl:
"God bless me! but the elephant
    Is nothing but a wall!"

The Second, feeling of the tusk,
    Cried: "Ho! what have we here
So very round and smooth and sharp?
    To me 'tis mighty clear
This wonder of an elephant
    Is very like a spear!"

The Third approached the animal,
    And, happening to take
the squirming trunk within his hands,
    Thus boldly up and spake:
"I see," quoth he, "the elephant
    Is very like a snake!"

The Fourth reached out his eager hand,
And felt about the knee:
"What most this wondrous beast is like
Is mighty plain," quoth he;
"'Tis clear enough the elephant
Is very like a tree."

The Fifth, who chanced to touch the ear,
Said: "E'en the blindest man
Can tell what this resembles most;
Deny the fact who can,
This marvel of an elephant
Is very like a fan!"

The Sixth no sooner had begun
About the beast to grope.
Than, seizing on the swinging tail
That fell within his scope,
"I see," quoth he, "the elephant
Is very like a rope!"

And so these men of Indostan
Disputed loud and long,
Each in his own opinion
Exceeding stiff and strong,
Though each was partly in the right,
And all were in the wrong!

So, oft in theologic wars
The disputants, I ween,
Rail on in utter ignorance
Of what each other mean,
And prate about an elephant
Not one of them has seen! [12]

All kidding aside, do you see the importance of relating complete details? Readers are like the six blind men of Indostan—if you don't give them enough information, they'll each jump to their own conclusions and won't be able to follow your story line.

Remember the phrase, "Show, don't tell." We reviewed many examples of this in previous chapters. By using specific details you can transport your reader to the scene of your story.

---

12. It should be noted, this stanza implies a false bias that theological truth is relative.

Example:

The pond was still—not a ripple marred its polished surface. The sun had set, but the moon had not yet risen. An eerie silence made the hair stand up on the back of my neck.

It was twilight, that time of day when all the earth seems to hold its breath. The thick foliage hung in the motionless air, and the smell of decay was strong. I strained to hear the whine of an insect or the reassuring creak of a cricket. But, all was silent. Even the birds held their chatter.

I watched the dim light fade … fade … fade.

SNAP!—a breaking twig shot the air with sound, causing my heart to stop, then triple its beat.

"Oh, did I scare you? Sorry."

I whirled around and gave my little brother a look of pure venom. Then, with a resigned sigh, I headed for the cabin. The mood was broken. I'd have to wait until tomorrow to find it again.

Were you able to picture this scene in your mind?

Notice how many senses I used to try to make you "see" the setting: sight, sound, smell, and touch.

I followed the "show, don't tell" rule by using phrases that demonstrated how nervous I was without my having to tell you ("An eerie silence made the hair stand up on the back of my neck," "the earth seems to hold its breath," "the smell of decay was strong").

- ❦ I used a "grabber" opening to arouse the reader's interest.
- ❦ I used onomatopoeia (SNAP!) to bring the scene to life.
- ❦ I used action words ("breaking twig shot the air," "I whirled around").
- ❦ I used every tool available to make the reader want to read on.
- ❦ Was I successful?

Let's see how famous authors handle descriptions:

The Story of Martin, The Cobbler

by Leo N. Tolstoy (1828–1910)

In a certain city of Russia dwelt Martin Avdyeeich, the cobbler. He lived in a cellar, a wretched little hole with a single window. The window looked up toward the street, and through it, Martin could just see the passers-by. It is true that he could see little more than their boots, but few indeed were the boots in that neighborhood which had not passed through his hands at some time or other. While Martin was still a journeyman, his wife had died, but she left him a little boy. No sooner had the little one begun to grow up and be a joy to his father's heart that he, too, died. Then, Martin grew so despondent that he began to murmur against God.

Lo! One day there came to him an aged peasant pilgrim. Martin fell a talking with him and began to complain of his great sorrow. "As for living any longer, thou man of God," said he, "I desire it not." But the man said to him, "Thy speech Martin, is not good. It is because thou wouldst fain have lived for thy own delight that thou does now despair."

❧ ❧

Review: In spite of the archaic language, did Tolstoy succeed in describing this scene? Did he make you see Martin's lowly dwelling. Did you *feel* Martin's pain? Look at the details: the cobbler lived in a cellar, "a wretched little hole" with one street-level window through which he watched the boots of passers-by—most of which he had made or repaired himself. His wife died while he was still learning his trade, and his son died some time later, leaving Martin alone and bitter.

You may have noticed that Tolstoy didn't follow paragraph and dialogue rules (he didn't start new paragraphs when the subject or speaker changed). Nor did he use a "grabber" opening sentence. However, keep in mind that he wrote this in the nineteenth century; composition rules weren't as strict then.

Robinson Crusoe

by Daniel DeFoe (1660–1731)

A little after noon, I found the sea very calm and the tide ebbed so far out that I could come within a quarter of a mile of the ship; and here I found a fresh renewing of my grief; for I saw, evidently, that if we had kept on board, we had all been safe; that is to say, we had all got safe on shore, and I would not have been so miserable as to be left entirely destitute of all comfort and company, as I now was.

This forced tears from my eyes again, but as there was little in that, I resolved, if possible to get to the ship; so I pulled off my clothes, for the weather was hot to extremity, and took to the water. But when I came to the ship, my difficulty was still greater to know how to get on board; for as she lay aground, and high out of the water, there was nothing within my reach to lay hold of.

I swam round her twice, and the second time I spied a small piece of rope, which I wondered I did not see at first, hanging down the forechains so low, as that with great difficulty I got hold of it, and by the help of that rope got up into the forecastle of the ship.

❧ ❧

Review: This well-known author chose to tell his story in the "first person" (I, me), rather than in the more common "third person" (he, she, it, they). There are restrictions when writing in the first person. For example, the central character tells the story and can only write from his personal observations of other characters or scenes. On the other hand, when writing in the third person, the writer, an unknown observer, freely switches from one character to another and from one scene to another.

DeFoe also broke several rules of composition: (a) He used words which were "telling, not showing"; (b) His first sentence (a full paragraph) is a whopping 90 words long! His last sentence (another full paragraph) is 56 words long. Our modern-day sentences should generally not exceed 20 words; (c) he used unnecessary words ("evidently," "that is to say").

Despite these problems, DeFoe's story has thrilled readers for centuries. A good story line or plot can overcome many technical problems or shortcomings.

Writers, always remember that people can't read your minds! Unless you describe your scene and character in some detail, no one else will be able to "see" it (don't forget "The Blind Men and the Elephant").

Descriptions should be written in active voice rather than passive voice:

Examples:

Active Voice:	We elected Johnny class president.
Passive Voice:	Johnny was elected class president.
Active Voice:	Mom drove me to the store.
Passive Voice:	I was driven to the store.

Can you see why active voice is preferred? It gives the reader more information and heightens his interest. It's more animated. Passive voice makes for dull reading and deadens the story's action.

Summary of Description Aids

❦ Use specific details to appeal to the senses: sight, sound, taste, touch, smell.

❦ Use figures of speech, fresh metaphors, and effective comparisons.

❦ Use vivid language—active verbs and explicit, definitive nouns; "show, don't tell": don't say "a bird sang"—say "a robin sang."

❦ Limit use of adverbs and adjectives: don't say "he walked quickly"—say "he fast-walked" or "he jogged."

❦ Omit unnecessary words.

❦ Use active voice rather than passive voice.

Writing Exercise

Write detailed descriptions on separate paper (at least 200 words each) for three of the following scenes. Although we've covered character development in Chapter Ten, don't worry about including or describing the characters here. Try to make the reader "see, hear, and feel" these settings.

1. Springtime at the zoo

2. A minor accident at a busy intersection

3. Opening day at the ball park

4. A physical description of your church

5. Your favorite restaurant on a holiday

6. A campground at Yellowstone Park

7. The inside of a courtroom

8. A dude ranch

Chapter Fourteen

Writing Dialogue

In creative writing, there are so many ways to make your story come alive. One of the most interesting ways is writing dialogue—creating conversations between two or more characters.

As you saw in Chapter Twelve, I use a great deal of dialogue in my stories. I've found that developing a story through conversation holds a reader's attention better than pure narration.

Narrative:

Susan adjusted the strap of her book bag and started jogging to the corner. She saw that the school bus was ready to drive away, so she yelled and ran faster. She thought to herself, if I'm late one more time, my name will be removed from the honor roll.

Dialogue:

"Wait for me!" Susan yelled, running and waving her arms to catch the bus driver's attention.

"Phew! That was close," she panted as she ran up the bus steps. "One more tardy slip and I lose my honor roll status."

Which example do you prefer? Both would be acceptable in a story, but the second example puts me in the character's shoes; I feel involved right from the start. Through Susan's words and actions, I experience her anxiety. The story seems vivacious, and I can envision the scene better. I find the first example dull by comparison.

Notice how I used action verbs: yelled, running, waving, panted, ran. I didn't weaken the action by inserting unnecessary adjectives and adverbs (limit the use of words like *very* and words ending in *-ly* because they lessen the impact of strong language).

Writing dialogue is easier than you might think. All you have to do is listen to people talk and write down what they say. Let's pretend we're overhearing a brief conversation at a grocery store:

Note: Be sure to identify the person speaking unless there are only two characters; in that case, you only need to identify one.

Example: "Excuse me."

"Yes, Ma'am?"

The clerk glanced at the bunch of bananas in the customer's hand.

"Yes, they just arrived today."

Were you able to follow this short exchange between the shopper and the grocery clerk? Although I didn't identify either speaker until the fourth line, you could easily determine who was speaking by the dialogue. Add a third person, however, and further identification becomes necessary.

Example: The clerk glanced at the bunch of bananas in the customer's hand.

"Yes, they just arrived today."

A young woman approached them and asked, "Could you tell me where I can find the carrots?"

"Certainly," the clerk replied, turning to point toward the vegetable bins lining the far wall. "The carrots are over there, between the tomatoes and the celery."

"Excuse me," the first customer said, tapping the clerk's shoulder. "How much do these bananas cost per pound?"

Rules for Writing Dialogue

There are several rules you need to know when writing dialogue:

1. Use quotation marks before and after a direct quotation or a character's exact words.

   Example: "Where's my book?" Paul asked.

2. Direct quotations begin with a capital letter.

   Example: "The play was wonderful," Susan said.

3. If a direct quotation is interrupted (a break in the quotation to identify the speaker), the second part of the quotation begins with a small letter.

   Example: "If we could," Janet added, "we'd give her my car."

   However, if a new sentence begins after the interruption, a capital letter would be used.

   Example: "I'll answer the phone," Buddy offered. "It's probably for me, anyway."

4. Commas, question marks, exclamation points, and periods are placed **inside** the closing quotation marks.

   Example: "I know I can do it," Scott said.

   "Are you sure?" Jessie asked.

   "Of course!" Scott nodded with confidence.

   "Well, let me know if you need help."

5. Start a new paragraph each time you change speakers.

> **Example:**   "I wish it was summer," Sarah said.
>
>   "Me, too!" Jeremy agreed.
>
>   "Me, three!" Lisa added with a laugh.

6. If there are several sentences within a quotation, place quotation marks only at the beginning and the end—do not enclose each sentence.

> **Example:**   "I thought it over," Molly said, "and I made my decision. You may use my new blouse tonight. But, in exchange, I want to borrow your pearl necklace."

7. If a character changes subjects during a direct quotation, (a) start a new paragraph with beginning quotation marks, and (b) place quotation marks only at the end of his entire discourse.

> **Example:**   "I was wrong," Dad admitted to Joe. "I'm sorry, son.
>
>   "Now, young lady," Dad turned to Anne with a stern look on his face, "what do you have to say for yourself?"

8. Use single quotation marks [' '] to enclose a quotation within a quotation.

> **Example:**   "Molly asked, 'What are you thinking about?' But, I didn't know what to say," Jason confessed.

9. Identify the speaker ("he said" = speaker ID) at a natural pause in the sentence; this normally occurs where a comma indicates a break.

> **Incorrect:**   "Of course, there's a difference in quality," he agreed, "and quantity."
>
> **Correct:**   "Of course," he agreed, "there's a difference in quality and quantity."
>
> **Incorrect:**   "In fact, I'm convinced," he added, "there's a market for his product."
>
> **Correct:**   "In fact," he added, "I'm convinced there's a market for his product."

10. To make your stories look more professional, vary the location of your speaker ID by placing it at the beginning, at the end, or in the middle of the character's speech.

> **Examples:**   (beginning)   *John said*, "Here I am."
>
>   (end)   "Here I am," *John said*.
>
>   (middle)   "Here I am," *John said*, "but not for long."

11. If you must identify your speaker, alternate the word *said* with a variety of synonyms to avoid repetition (often referred to as "echoing").

> **Examples:**
>
> | he said | Donnie sputtered | Casey snapped |
> |---|---|---|
> | John added | Mary remarked | Brenda whispered |
> | Jake agreed | Gloria declared | Denise gushed |

Sarah yelled	she howled	Carol giggled
Janet cried	Kim sobbed	Angie quoted
Bob shouted	Annie muttered	Philip announced

12. Avoid speaker ID whenever possible by using identifying dialogue and action instead.

Example A: "Every time I see your room, it upsets me."

"Mom, I promise I'll clean my room after dinner."

"That's what you said yesterday."

"But, this time I really mean it!"

Example B: Janet sighed. "I don't know what's wrong with me. I'm so tired."

Chris looked at her friend in concern. "Do you think you're coming down with the flu?"

"I hope not."

"Maybe you should take a nap instead of going shopping this afternoon."

Janet rubbed her puffy eyes and stifled a yawn. "I think you're right," she agreed.

13. Avoid writing dialogue which uses phonetics or dialects.

Example: "He was runnin' away cuz he was skeered of gettin' spanked."

It's difficult to read and it's extremely difficult for an author to maintain the same dialect throughout his composition. Instead, use good grammar for clarity and show geographic identity through descriptions and actions.

Example: "Perhaps I should go indoors now," Phoebe said. Her cheeks were already pink from the sun, even though she wore a hat to protect her fair Irish complexion.

Let's study the following Bible passages which include dialogue:

Example A: The wife of a man from the company of the prophets cried out to Elisha, [13] "Your servant my husband is dead, and you know that he revered the Lord. But now his creditor is coming to take my two boys as his slaves." [14]

[15] Elisha replied to her, [16] "How can I help you? Tell me, what do you have in your house?"

"Your servant has nothing there at all," she said, "except a little oil." [17]

Elisha said, "Go around and ask all your neighbors for empty jars. Don't ask for just a few. Then go inside and shut the door behind you and your sons. Pour oil into all the jars, and as each is filled, put it to one side" [18] (2 Kings 4:1–4 [NIV]).

---

13. Rule 10 (alternate location of speaker ID)
14. Rule 6 (multi-sentence quotation marks at beginning and end of entire discourse)
15. Rule 5 (start new paragraph with change of speakers)
16. Rule 11 (use synonyms in place of "said")
17. Rule 3 (use small letter to begin second half of interrupted quotation)
18. Rule 1 (use quotation marks before and after a direct quote)

Example B: Simon Peter asked him,[19] "Lord, where are you going?"[20]

Jesus replied, [21]"Where I am going, you cannot follow now, but you will follow later."[22]

Peter asked, "Lord, why can't I follow you now? I will lay down my life for you."[23]

Then Jesus answered, [24]"Will you really lay down your life for me? I tell you the truth, before the rooster crows, you will disown me three times!

[25]"Do not let your hearts be troubled. Trust in God; trust also in me. In my Father's house are many rooms … I am going there to prepare a place for you" (John 13:36–14:2 [NIV]).

Summary of Dialogue Rules

- ❦ Use quotation marks before and after a direct quote.

- ❦ Begin direct quotes with a capital letter.

- ❦ Use a small letter to begin the second part of an interrupted quotation. If a new sentence begins after the interruption, use a capital letter.

- ❦ Punctuation marks are placed inside the closing quotation marks.

- ❦ Start a new paragraph with each change of speaker.

- ❦ Multi-sentence quotes require quotation marks only at the beginning and at the end of the entire discourse.

- ❦ When a speaker changes subjects, (a) start a new paragraph with beginning quotation marks, (b) place end quotation marks only at the end of a complete quote.

- ❦ Use single quotation marks [' '] to enclose a quotation within a quotation.

- ❦ Identify the speaker at a natural pause in the sentence.

- ❦ Alternate the location of the speaker ID.

- ❦ Use synonyms in place of "said" to avoid tiresome repetition.

- ❦ Whenever possible, use dialogue, description, and action to identify the speaker in place of speaker ID.

- ❦ Avoid using phonetics or dialect.

---

19. Rule 10 (alternate location of speaker ID)
20. Rule 4 (place punctuation marks inside the closing quotation marks)
21. Rule 2 (begin direct quotes with a capital letter)
22. Rule 1 (use quotation marks before and after a direct quote)
23. Rule 6 (multi-sentence quotation marks at beginning and end of entire discourse)
24. Rule 10 (alternate location of speaker ID)
25. Rule 7 (start new paragraph when speaker changes subjects; use beginning quotation marks; ending quotation marks only at the end of complete quote)

Writing Exercise

Select three dialogue-filled passages of approximately the same length as the earlier examples (either from the Bible or from literature). Write out the passages, then make a list of the dialogue rules used for each. You may refer to the dialogue rules by their number only. Please use separate paper if additional space is needed.

_____

_____

_____

_____

_____

_____

_____

_____

_____

_____

_____

_____

_____

_____

_____

_____

_____

_____

_____

_____

_____

Chapter Fifteen

The Moment of Truth

$\mathcal{A}$fter reading the chapter on outlining, you know that a climax is a traumatic moment or turning point in the action and is located near the end of the story. It's the occasion of highest dramatic tension and always has a major impact on the central character. It's the moment of truth.

This climatic scene may take many forms. The following are examples of turning points taken from short stories I've written which have been accepted by various publishing houses:[26]

///

Sisters

Megan turned around and saw that Jessica was holding her throat with both hands, and her face was turning dark red! "Jessica!" Megan cried, jumping to her feet.

Jessica couldn't breathe. Her mouth was open, but she couldn't seem to get air. Her girlfriends cried out. "Help her, someone!"

Megan grabbed Jessica by the arm and pulled her from the booth onto the floor. With Jessie slumped over on her hands and knees, Megan quickly stood behind her and encircled Jessica's waist with her arms. She formed a fist with her left hand and grabbed it with her right hand. Then, she pulled up as hard as she could, pressing against Jessie's diaphragm, performing the Heimlich maneuver she had seen on a public television program a few nights before. With determined concentration, Megan pulled, and pulled. When she pulled up a third time, suddenly a piece of hamburger flew out of Jessica's mouth.

Jessie sucked in several deep breaths and coughed. Then, she removed Megan's arms from her waist and sat on the floor, breathing hard. Finally, her face turned a more natural shade.

Jessica looked at Megan through watery eyes. "You saved my life!" she said wonderingly. She looked up at the people standing around them and repeated, "She saved my life!"

Note: This was the turning point in the relationship between two sisters.

---

26. The stories excerpted in chapters 15 and 16 are published by Christian Liberty Press unless otherwise indicated.

The Phantom Driver[27]

The night was quiet. Ken and I sat on the edge of our chairs on the front porch, eyes turned in the direction the driver normally came from, ears straining to hear the car's engine echoing from the next street. 2:30 a.m. came and went—no sign of him. 2:45 a.m. passed quietly. Ken whispered, "I hope Bob doesn't give up yet." We couldn't see Bob's car parked around the corner, but we knew it was there.

Suddenly, we heard the faint hum of a car engine! Seconds later, lights were flickering on the trees. "Here he comes!" Ken said, grimly. "The Phantom Driver" came into view, interior overhead light glowing, highway lights piercing the dark empty streets.

As usual, he made a U-turn in front of our house. I imagined I could hear the whirring of Jane's video camera recording the incident. "The Phantom" made a left turn and drove past Bob's parked car. Bob ignited the engine, turned on his lights, and followed slowly behind, leaving just enough distance between them so the driver wouldn't know he was being followed. We watched their lights until we couldn't see them any longer.

The night passed.

Note: This is a pivotal scene in a suspense story.

The Braggart

"Good luck, James," Jennifer whispered. "I hope you win!"

James turned to look at her suspiciously. What did she mean by that, he wondered? Why would she want him to win? He could tell she needed the money by the faded dress she was wearing.

Mr. Levi cleared his throat and spoke into the microphone, calling for silence. He asked Jennifer a question about literature. Jennifer sat thoughtfully, then she answered in her soft voice.

"Correct!"

Mr. Levi looked at James. "Name the author of *The Count of Monte Cristo.*"

All of a sudden, James's mind went blank! The only thing he could think of was Jennifer's comment, "Good luck, James … I hope you win!"

James leaned forward, but the answer didn't blurt out, as usual. Then, he heard the timer buzz and he heard Mr. Levi say, "I'm sorry, but your time is up." From a distance, he heard Mr. Levi ask Jennifer the same question and heard Jennifer's soft response, "Alexandre Dumas."

Note: This scene had a life-changing impact on James.

---

27. Published by Whispers & Shouts, Creative Reading, Sandpoint Newsline, Se La Vie, and Anterior.

A Lesson Well-Learned

As Kandi walked Annie to her friend's house across the street, Mother thought, once more, of how grateful she was for her 12-year-old daughter's help. Kandi was so capable and responsible for her age. Mother couldn't imagine what it would have been like, trying to take care of the new baby and Annie without her.

Kandi returned and started warming a bottle of formula while her mother finished bathing the baby.

"She's so tiny!" Kandi exclaimed. "She looks just like Annie, only smaller." She laughed as the baby grabbed her finger in a tight grip.

Just then, they heard a piercing scream!

Eyes wide with fear, Mother shoved the baby into Kandi's arms and ran to the front door. Her neighbor's oldest daughter rushed to meet her, shouting, "A dog attacked Annie! Hurry!"

Note: Obviously, this traumatic scene impacted Kandi's life.

The Unlikely Heroes

Alan gave Bobbie a hard push, and the smaller boy slid through the open window.

"I'm kneeling in the sink," Bobbie said from inside. "There's smoke coming from the front of the house, and the smoke detector's blaring." Bobbie turned to look at Alan and said, "I'm going to let the dog out now. She's laying on the floor and looks pretty sick. You run to Jimmy's house and call the fire department."

"Okay!" Alan agreed, turning and running as fast as he could to the brown house three doors away.

In the meantime, Bobbie climbed down from the sink to the kitchen floor and opened the back door. He coughed from the heavy gray smoke entering his lungs as he bent over to pick up the miniature collie. The dog's tail wagged limply, and she licked Bobbie's face as he carried her out of the smoke-filled house and gently laid her on the grass in the backyard.

Just then, Alan ran around the corner and yelled. "They're on the way! How's the dog? Are there any other animals inside?"

"I don't know," Bobbie called as Alan stuck his head inside the back door and started whistling.

Without warning, a black cat streaked past Alan's legs and raced to where the collie was lying. As Alan ran to join Bobbie and the animals, he heard the distant whine of the fire engine.

Note: Rescue scenes are great climactic moments.

Corey and the Bumblebee

Corey was perched on his bike seat, leaning against the house with one hand and gripping the bicycle handle with the other, moving slowly back and forth. He was deep in thought and didn't notice the buzzing around his head at first.

Suddenly, he felt a slight breeze and a loud buzzing next to his right ear. He turned his head and there, not two inches from his face, was the largest bumblebee Corey had ever seen in his life!

"Get away!" Corey yelled, but the insect just flew around to his left ear.

Corey ducked forward and felt the bee brush against the back of his head.

"Mom, a giant bee is after me!" he cried, but his mother was removing clothes from the dryer in the basement and didn't hear him.

Corey watched in horror as the huge bee landed on his left hand, which was resting against the wall of the house.

Instinctively, he flicked his left hand, grabbed his bicycle handle, and threw all his weight on his right pedal. Without thinking, Corey started pedaling frantically down the driveway and out onto the empty street.

Note: Corey's fear of the bee was greater than his fear of riding a bicycle; this became a dramatic turning point for him.

Gotcha!

It was dark and quiet, and Tony's eyelids closed and his head was just beginning to sag when the familiar humming sound started once more. He jerked upright and scanned the sky for signs of life.

Suddenly, Tony saw a circle of flashing golden lights coming from the open field behind his house!

"Dad, they're landing!" Tony's voice was high-pitched from fear. This time, he didn't wait for his father to come; he ran gladly to the safety of his parents' bedroom.

"They're landing in the field behind the house!" Tony shouted as he pulled his father's hand. "Believe me, I'm telling the truth! You've got to believe me, this time! I swear, I'll never lie or play tricks again! But, hurry! Please, Dad, hurry!"

"Do you mean it?" his father asked, sitting on the edge of his bed. "You'll never lie or play jokes on people again?"

"I promise, Dad!" Tony said fervently. "Hurry!"

Tony's father followed him to his bedroom and looked out the window. The flashing golden lights were still there.

Note: Fear also produces great climactic scenes.

They Called Her "Annie Oakley"

"Help me!" Jimmy shrieked. He was so frightened, he couldn't move.

"Mom, the dogs are coming!" I cried.

My mother came running from the house with my Daisy B-B rifle in her hand.

"You children go inside!" she ordered. "And don't come out until I tell you it's all right!" She paused long enough to see that we obeyed her, then she ran down the steps toward Jimmy.

The dogs were only three houses away by the time Mom reached him. She took Jimmy's arm and pulled him behind her, then she raised the B-B rifle and started shooting at them.

YELP! The pellets struck the rump of a German shepherd. Then an Irish setter was hit on the shoulder. The pack skidded to a stop twenty feet from where Mom and Jimmy stood. A feisty terrier looked around at the other dogs in confusion, then he barked at Mom and started advancing toward her. Mom fired a B-B into the street in front of him, and the terrier backed up.

The leader barked, and the pack suddenly turned and started running back up the street.

Mom hit two more backsides as they retreated. Then, she grabbed Jimmy's arm and ran with him up our front steps and into the house.

Note: This climax scene combines action, fear, and rescue.

The Baby Is Missing

Mark studied the latest picture of Kasey, which was sitting on the dresser. He had never noticed the little cleft in her chin before. It looked just like his own chin! And her bright little eyes were sky blue, just like his mother's. Mark began to feel a constriction around the area of his heart. He wished he had shown her some attention. As he glanced away from her picture, his gaze fell on the small white Bible the pastor had given Kasey as a present. Mark's mother read to the baby from the little Bible every day. She said Kasey liked the sound of her voice, and you never knew how much a baby understood.

Mark picked up the small Bible and flipped through the pages. He recognized some of the stories he had read in Bible study. As he skimmed through the parables, Mark began to realize how selfish he had been, acting so cool and distant to his family during the past few months. If they found Kasey, he vowed that he would make it up to her, and to his parents.

Note: A climax can be a quiet moment of enlightenment.

A Matter of Trust[28]

Emily glanced at her watch. It seemed to be taking Lucas an exceptionally long time to help Juanita into her wheelchair! While Joe talked, Emily had heard little exclamations and strange noises coming from Juanita's room. Just when she decided to see what was keeping them, Emily heard the distinct sound of rubber wheels on tile approaching from that direction.

"Wait a minute!" Emily snapped as she stepped in front of Lucas and the old woman. She looked down at Juanita Johnson and stopped—staring in open-mouthed astonishment.

The elderly Alzheimer patient was clutching a blanket-wrapped doll to her thin chest, rocking back and forth in her wheelchair, and humming softly. Then she looked up at Emily and said, "Lucas found my little Janie! Here's my girl, at last!" Then, she broke into a beautiful smile and rubbed her cheek against the doll's head, humming once more.

Emily felt paralyzed with shock. Not once, in all the years that she had been head nurse at Swann's Nursing Home, had she seen Juanita Johnson smile—much less sing!

Note: Enlightenment can come in many ways; this moment changed Emily's outlook on life forever.

Half-Empty, Half-Full[29]

"So what!" Christine replied bitterly. "People can't change their personalities."

"Of course they can!" Jessica's face lit up with a smile. "It's like changing a habit. Instead of dwelling on the negative, you try to find something positive to focus on. It's your choice!" Jessie turned to face the window again. "For instance, what do you see when you look out this window?"

Chris looked through the window and said, "Snow."

"Find something good to say about it," Jessica encouraged her. "Look at the way it coats the trees. It's almost like a work of art, isn't it?"

Chris looked outside again. "Well … it does look kind of pretty … if you like snow!" The corners of her mouth turned up in the beginning of a smile. It transformed her face.

"See what I mean?" Jessica crowed triumphantly. She turned and pointed to the kitchen table. "What do you see there?"

"I see an empty …" Chris caught herself, "I mean, I see a cereal bowl waiting to be filled."

"Yes, that's it!" Jessie impulsively threw her arms around Christine's shoulders and hugged her. She let her arms drop when she felt Chris stiffen. "I'm sorry, I guess I got carried away."

Note: Again, a life-changing moment can be quiet.

---

28. Published by *Back Porch Magazine*.
29. Published by Word Aflame Publications.

As you can see, a story climax can be physical, mental, or emotional. It can involve rescues, suspense, moral dilemmas, spiritual awakenings, accidents, fear, shame, or any combination of these and more. But, whatever the conflict and climax, it must impact the central character's life.

Writing Exercise

Review the last two novels you have read and find the climactic moments in both of them. Copy the entire scene in which each climax takes place in the space below, then keep them handy—they'll serve as additional examples for your future reference.

You might consider starting a "Climax Journal" in which you'd keep copies of dramatic scenes that made a great impression on you when you read them. This is just one more tool that a writer can use to help himself create exciting fictional stories.

Climax Scene One

Book Title: _____

_____

_____

_____

_____

_____

_____

Climax Scene Two

Book Title: _____

_____

_____

_____

_____

_____

_____

Chapter Sixteen

End with a Bang!

*H*ow do you feel when you finish a short story or a novel? Are you happy, inspired, and satisfied, or depressed, angry, disappointed, and confused? Obviously, your feelings depend a great deal on the subject matter, plot, conflict, climax, and the writer's ability.

Have you ever read a really good story that you greatly enjoyed, but it seemed to fizzle out at the end—as if the author got tired of writing the story and just stopped? I think we've all had that experience, and it's very disappointing. Sometimes, it even makes you angry—you feel like you have wasted your time. That's how important a good ending is. There's a right way and a wrong way to finish writing a story. Hopefully, this chapter will help you find the right way.

Powerful or surprise endings are very effective in story closure (of course, nothing works if your story is not interesting and well-written from the beginning). Humor is another popular ending tool. A reader should walk away from your story with a blessing, a smile, some biblical truth worthwhile to think about, or a new outlook that applies to the Word of God. Whatever you do, don't let your story die for lack of a good conclusion.

Let's review a few examples of selected endings taken from my short stories:

Mail Order Bride[30]

After pounding on the bolted door for several minutes, Brother Jake walked around to the window and scraped a small, circular area to look through.

Later, he would tell the townsfolk that he couldn't close his eyes without seeing the picture of Big John McDougal, frozen solid, sitting upright, eyes open, with one arm around his young daughter and the other arm around his mail-order bride.

They were buried that way, near the cabin. Eventually, a memorial stone was erected to mark the spot. Then, in 1896, gold was discovered in

---

30. Published by Creative Reading and Advocate.

the Yukon. The cabin was occupied by several different trappers and prospectors, until it burned down one particularly cold night. Rumor had it that no one stayed in that cabin very long. Some people say that the last occupant set fire to it himself, screaming, "Go away!" as he ran out into the snow.

Note: This is known as a "shocking ending"—especially effective in suspense thrillers and mysteries.

The Phantom Driver[31]

'The Phantom' made a left turn and drove past Bob's dark car. Bob ignited the engine, turned on his lights, and followed slowly behind, leaving just enough distance between them so the driver wouldn't know he was being followed. We watched their lights until we couldn't see them any longer.

The night passed.

Early the next morning, we heard the news: Bob was able to see 'The Phantom Driver's' license plate numbers clearly. Also, the driver had driven around every cul-de-sac in the neighborhood—in the opposite direction! Then Bob saw him throw something out of his window! This happened several times until the realization dawned on Bob: "The Phantom Driver" was … a *Journal Newspaper* delivery man!

Note: Surprise endings catch the reader off-guard.

The Grass Isn't Always Greener …

Jessica was stunned! It couldn't be true. Mr. and Mrs. Thomas had always been so fun-loving and carefree. They always seemed so nice, and Jessica had envied Janie her free lifestyle. Now, the Thomases were getting a divorce and sending Janie away!

Jessica thought about what her mother had told her that morning, 'We wouldn't be so protective of you if we didn't love you.' Could it be possible that she had been so mistaken? Jessica thought of how her father's eyes lit up when he saw her. She thought of the little, special things her mother did for her, like ironing the pleats on her favorite skirt so they would lay properly, and drawing little smiling hearts on her telephone messages. She tried to imagine what it would be like to be in Janie's shoes and face the possibility of losing her parents.

Jessica shuddered and tightened her arm around Janie's shoulders. "Put some clothes in your school bag," she told the heartbroken girl. "You're coming home with me tonight."

While Jessica waited for her best friend to pack her clothes, she thought of how hard she was going to hug her mother when she got home.

Note: Thought-provoking endings can be powerful.

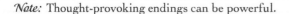

31. Published by Whispers & Shouts, Creative Reading, Sandpoint Newsline, Se La Vie, and Anterior.

The Unlikely Heroes

By Monday morning, Alan and Bobbie were famous! Not only had they saved the Flanders' beloved pets, but they had saved their home, too. Apparently, Mr. Flanders had thrown his newspaper too close to the cooling fireplace when he left for work that morning, and the glowing coals had set it on fire. The family room was pretty heavily damaged, but the rest of the house was saved—thanks to the two young boys.

Alan and Bobbie received commendations from the Fire Department, which were given to them by the Mayor at a special ceremony on Sunday. Their pictures were in the weekend newspaper, and they were presented with money certificates by Mr. and Mrs. Flanders.

But, best of all, they were heroes to everyone at school. The other boys started asking them to join their games, and it turned out that Alan was the best football guard the school team had ever seen, and Bobbie was the fastest goalie the hockey team ever had!

Alan and Bobbie were still known as "Mutt and Jeff," but now their classmates said it proudly, as if it was a badge of honor … just like the awards the two unlikely heroes received.

Note: This is a 'feel-good' ending; the title came from the final paragraph.

Gotcha!

"The second lesson is, continually playing jokes on people is like lying to them. They learn not to trust you. So, even if you had seen a UFO, we would have found it impossible to believe you, unless we saw it with our own eyes. Do you understand now?"

Tony looked from face to face around the kitchen table. Not one of them was smiling; they wore serious, concerned expressions. His initial surprise had turned to anger, and now to chagrin. He had never given a thought to his victims before. Was this how they felt, he wondered?

Tony looked down at the table as a wave of shame swept over him.

"You're right, Dad," Tony said at last. "I never realized how it felt on the receiving end, until now. I'm really sorry. I'll never do it again. I promise … again!"

Everyone broke into smiles then. Tony's mother went to the stove to heat up some hot chocolate, while Johnny explained how he had worked the miniature flying saucer he borrowed from his cousin.

There was a sense of profound relief all around.

Note: Sometimes, I try to end with a life-changing message—hopefully without sounding too didactic [preachy].

Behold the Face of My Father

"You can go in to see him now," the doctor added.

When Katie saw her little brother's broken body encased in casts and surrounded by beeping instruments, her eyes filled with tears again.

They approached Ricky, carefully avoiding his suspended right arm and leg. He was as white as his sheets, his head was bandaged, and the skin around both eyes was discolored.

As Katie looked at his sweet, wide face, the words floated into her mind, "Despise not these little ones…. Behold the face of my Father…." Katie closed her eyes and prayed, "Lord, forgive me for my past mistakes. I promise to love and care for Ricky, as long as I live. Thank you for giving him back to us." When she opened her eyes, Hannah was smiling at her. Hannah knew. And Katie somehow knew that Hannah would be there for her, every step of the way.

"I want to know more about the Bible and about God's love," Katie thought. Then and there, she decided that she, too, would join the teen Bible study group. And, when Ricky was well, she would take him with her! She'd never turn away from him again!

With newfound peace, Katie smiled back at Hannah. Then she heard a small voice say, "Hi, Kat!"

Note: I try to close my stories with realistic, satisfactory, and inspirational endings whenever possible.

Blessed Are the Peacemakers[32]

"Instead of becoming angry, I told Sarah how much it hurt me to be left out, and she apologized. So, we're still best friends. You should give Christopher a chance, too. Tell him how you felt when he said … whatever he said. Talk it over. Fighting never solved anything."

"But, I already gave him a chance to take it back—twice—and he wouldn't!"

"Phillip, I think you're overreacting. What exactly did Christopher say that's so terrible?"

"He told me you'd never win the Miss Homecoming Queen Pageant because you're too ugly! He said his sister's going to win instead!"

DeeDee's eyebrows shot up with surprise. After a moment, she started looking around the kitchen. "Where are those boxing gloves?" she asked. "I'm going to punch him in the nose, too!"

Then, she laughed to show she was just kidding.

Phillip slowly grinned. He had to admit, it did sound pretty funny—once he thought about it. Maybe he'd give his best friend another chance, after all.

Note: I use humorous endings as often as possible.

---

32. Published by V.R. Williams and Whispers & Shouts.

Whoa, Car![33]

Grandma stopped rocking and looked at the children knowingly. "Everyone else thought the car took off by itself," she said, "but I knew better. Your Grandpa Vernie was a proud man, and he just wanted to prove that he could drive it, alone—without his cousin's help." She chuckled and sat back, once more rocking slowly.

"Well, it was quite a sight.... Vernie was hanging onto the steering wheel with a shocked look on his face. The clouds of dust made it hard for his cousin to see where he went, but the rest of us were standing up on the front porch and we could see Vernie making wide circles around the barn. After a few minutes, he knew he was in trouble; he'd mastered the skill of driving, all right, but he'd forgotten to ask how to stop! His cousin continued to shout instructions to Vernie, but that old car was so noisy that Vernie couldn't hear him."

Grandma laughed softly at the memory. "But, you know, we could hear Vernie's voice above the racket. He was shouting, 'Whoa, car! Whoa there, old car!' as if he was talking to our old plow horse!"

The children laughed, delightedly, and the adults who had entered the room while the story was in progress were laughing in appreciation, too. "I remember that story," Uncle Eddie said, nodding.

"But, Grandma, how did Grandpa Vernie finally stop the car?" Scott asked when the laughter had died down.

"Well, he just rode around and around until it ran out of gas—which was close to midnight!" Grandma replied with a grin.

Once again, the room was filled with laughter ... and memories.

Note: A combination of humorous and surprise endings can be very effective.

Learning To Trust

Deborah Rogers shook her head with wonder at the strength Buck exhibited. "Surely, God must have sent this animal to us," she thought to herself. They began the slow, tedious, uphill process, and she guided the wheelchair around tree limbs and rocks as Buck pulled. Gradually, her mind began to wander. "Your birthday is only a week from today," she reflected at one point.

Buck's ears twitched backward, but he continued to strain toward the crest of the hill without stopping.

"That's it, Buck! Keep going! Good boy!" Becky urged as they approached the edge. One final tug, and the wheelchair was back on the hiking trail once more.

As soon as they stabilized the wheelchair, Becky and her mother both threw their arms around the panting animal. Becky rubbed her face in his luxurious fur and said, "Thank you, Buck. You're such a good boy!" Then she reached her mother's hand. "I'm really sorry I worried you, Mom. From now on, I'll wait until Ryan or one of my friends can come with me before I go 'hiking,' again."

---

33. Published by Life Enrichment, Advocate, and Christian Liberty Press.

Becky's mother smiled with relief. "No need to lecture Becky," she thought, "she's learning as she goes."

"Okay, Buck, let's go home. Pull!" Becky glanced over to her mother. Her mother guided the wheelchair as Buck pulled her along the dirt path. "Now, what were you saying about my birthday?" she asked, grinning.

Note: Positive endings are inspirational.

The Prevaricator

Brian was slumped in the chair with his head hanging down. Slowly, he straightened up, swallowed, and met Mrs. Tripp's eyes. "I lied about my employment record because I was afraid you wouldn't hire me without experience." Brian's cheeks burned. "I guess Uncle Dan told you the truth," he stated, rather than asked.

"Frankly, I haven't had time to check on your references yet. I was simply asking about your skills and abilities—what you had written down was illegible."

Brian's eyes widened as he realized what she was saying. If he hadn't confessed to falsifying some of the information on his employment application, he might have gotten away with it. But then he shook his head, knowing that he couldn't have continued to live with himself. He longed to get back into a good relationship with the Lord; he missed his former, easygoing, open life. He'd found out that living a lie wasn't worth the sacrifice.

"Obviously, I must terminate your employment," Mrs. Tripp added, interrupting his thoughts. The disappointment in her eyes cut Brian deeply. "And the chance of your being employed here in the future is very slim."

"Yes, Ma'am, I understand." Brian nodded and rose to his feet as she dismissed him.

As he collected his personal belongings and final paycheck, Brian rehearsed in his mind how he would tell his uncle and parents about his transgression. The only way he could avoid it would be to tell lie after lie, to explain the loss of his job. And, as Brian had discovered, there is no peace in prevarication.

Note: Hopefully, this ending will give readers something to think about; also, reinforcing the title and main theme in the final paragraph emphasizes your message.

Summary

In closing, let me repeat that a story ending must satisfy your reader. Remember how you feel when you read an unsatisfactory ending—cheated! Keep that in mind when writing your final paragraphs. As I said earlier, try to leave your reader with a blessing, a smile, something worthwhile to think about, or a new outlook. If you succeed, they'll want to read more of your work—and editors will want to publish it.

Writing Exercise

Choose two short stories or novels that you've read recently and write down their endings. Then, study them—as well as any other story ending that amuses, intrigues, or inspires you. These will serve as standards that you should aim for. Use them as examples and learn from them.

Once again, you may want to start an "Endings Journal" that will include a variety of successful endings for future reference.

Chapter Seventeen

Ready to Write!

*A*t last! It's time to begin writing your story!

Gather your pen, paper, and notes on beginnings, dialogue, narrative, plots, outlines, character sketches, climaxes, and endings. Find a quiet corner where you can write undisturbed. Then review your chosen plot, outline, and character sketches once more—and read through the following before you begin to write.

1. *Pray for guidance and inspiration before you begin to write and throughout the entire process.*

Ask God to guide your thoughts and your pen so you will create a written work that will bless, inspire, entertain, and teach—a work that will glorify His name. I always prepare for writing by saying this prayer, and I've found that the Lord honors my request. We've gone into more detail on this subject in Chapter Seven, "Write in the Light."

2. *For your first draft, don't worry about spelling, punctuation, or even grammar and composition.*

The important thing is to get your story down on paper. We'll discuss rewriting and proofreading in later chapters.

3. *Be spontaneous—turn your imagination loose!*

Visualize your characters and scenes in your mind. Listen to what your characters say and write it down. This is the exciting part of writing—slipping into other personalities and living their adventures on paper.

4. *Pretend you're describing a scene to a friend who is blindfolded.*

He can't see what you are looking at, so you must be explicit in your descriptions. It's the same with dialogue—no one can hear what your characters say until you write down their words. Let their dialogue flow smoothly, back and forth between characters, the way it does between you and your friends or family.

Creating a story is as simple as that—you begin with an idea, develop a plot and an outline, "flesh out" your characters, visualize the scenes, and write them down.

5. *Keep writing as long as the words come freely.*

If writing becomes difficult or stressful, take a break and review your outline and characters again. If that doesn't get your creative juices flowing once more, put your story aside for a while. But try to get back to it as soon as possible. Don't procrastinate—write while it's still fresh in your mind. Delay will only make writing your story more difficult. Remember, this is only your first draft; you can rewrite later, so be as creative as you can.

6. *You may notice some strange things happening as you write.*

Your central character may begin to develop a personality totally unlike the one you prepared for him! If so, change the character sketch to match the emerging personality. Likewise, your story may take an entirely new turn. This frequently happens when a story comes to life. If it happens to you, change your outline and follow the new direction to its conclusion. This is normal in story writing. As you progress, step by step, your story may take twists and turns you didn't foresee when you first wrote the outline. Your original outline is not carved in stone—it's merely a map to guide you from one point to another. Don't be afraid to change directions. Explore this new journey to its outcome—it will probably be much better than the one you had originally planned. If not, you can always revise it in the rewrite stage.

7. *Write the entire story without stopping to edit or correct the earlier portion.*

Trying to proofread your story before it's done will squash your creativity. Imagine what would happen if a chef decided to wash his pots and pans and clean up the kitchen between each entree—the meal might never be finished!

8. *Let your unique, natural "voice" come through.*

Don't try to imitate other writers—be yourself! How would the real "you" write? Exactly the way you sound when you speak. Your writing style, or "voice," may be poetic and filled with dialogue, or abrupt, using short sentences and lots of narrative. Just as everyone has a distinct personality, each person has a different way of expressing themselves on paper. You will discover your individual style as you continue writing. It may be a little vague, at first, but it will shine through eventually.

9. *Use concrete nouns and active verbs.*

The use of adjectives and adverbs is necessary, but try to use them as little as possible. It's better to use good solid verbs and nouns, strong words that say exactly what you mean without having to strengthen them with adverbs and adjectives. However, don't waste time worrying about it as you write your first draft; we'll save the bulk of this kind of detail for the rewriting and proofreading stages. But try to get into the habit of thinking in terms of strong, descriptive words. It will give your story more impact and save you time in the long run.

10. *Too much fat is bad for your story.*

Don't be too descriptive and flowery or your composition might become unpalatable and hard to digest. Have you ever read something that was so sickeningly sweet or overwritten that you had to put it down?

Learn from that experience and don't subject your readers to that type of excess. Also, remember to use plain English and common words (don't use fifty-cent words where nickel words will do). Save your lyrical language for writing poetry where it can be more appreciated.

11. Don't bite off more than you can chew.

Don't try to tackle a novel as your first written work. To begin with, write short stories of 800-1,000 words (3-4 double-spaced pages). You'll find that each story has its own length. Write until the story reaches its natural outcome. It would be wise, however, to save complicated, longer plots until you have some writing experience behind you.

12. Write about what you know.

Unless you plan to spend a great deal of time researching your subject, write about something you are familiar with. Eventually you will want to expand into new territory but wait until you are more experienced in creative writing. You can't fake your way through a story; today's readers are too well-traveled and intelligent. And don't worry about being too young or not having enough life experiences to write interesting stories. Some of the most fascinating tales ever written were about dogs, country living, one-room schoolhouses, growing up, and the like. You don't have to be worldly and sophisticated to write a masterpiece—but you do have to be knowledgeable about your subject.

13. Enjoy yourself.

Have fun with your writing. Get into the spirit of the composition and allow yourself to enjoy the experience. Writing is very satisfying and can be great fun. Of course, your topic has a lot to do with your feelings: if you are writing about illness or death, it's no laughing matter. But if you can move your readers with your words, it's a blessing to both of you. Laugh and cry with your characters; what you feel will be reflected in your writing.

14. Don't be over exuberant!

I have a tendency to overuse exclamatory sentences and interjections (Wow!)—have you noticed? I must rein myself in, at times, in order to control my enthusiasm. That's my personality—my "voice"—but it can be very tiresome to a reader when it's overdone. And when something is excessive, it's less effective, or even counter-productive. If you don't want to lose your reader, use interjections and exclamatory sentences only at appropriate times, when they are absolutely needed to advance or intensify the story.

15. Don't lecture people through your composition.

If your stories preach, dictate, or in any way lecture readers, you will lose them. Heavy-handed writing turns people away. Instead, educate through your plots. Give examples of how Christians overcome their struggles. Show your characters facing and resolving their conflicts through prayer and by obeying God's Word. But their resolution must be realistic to be effective. Preaching should be left to ordained ministers and controversy is better addressed in a nonfiction forum—like a letter to the editor, a well-written article, or a town hall meeting.

16. Leave something to the reader's imagination.

Don't try to explain every detail in your story. Assume that the reader has a reasonable amount of intelligence. This is especially important when writing dialogue; some writers think they have to identify every speaker. As we noted in Chapter Fourteen, there are other ways of letting the reader know who's speaking besides adding, "he said." That holds true in your narrative, as well. "Show, don't tell." If you want to describe an overweight shopper, for instance, you might say, "He huffed and puffed heavily down the aisle." Readers want to use their imagination; otherwise, they would be watching a movie instead of reading your story.

17. Write clearly.

Don't confuse the reader through vagueness, or by using dialect or "street language." Write in plain, standard English, and in a way that can be easily understood. Be original in *what* you say, not in *how* you say it. Some politicians are deliberately obscure when they're trying to win votes; they have been known to "talk around the issues." As a writer, your goal is to inspire, entertain, teach, or bless the reader—not bewilder him. So, use language that sounds natural through the use of plain English, good grammar, contractions, nouns and verbs, strengthening adjectives and adverbs, and figures of speech (sparingly). Write clearly, don't make up your own words, and don't use slang or unclear phrases.

Writing Exercise

On separate paper, write the first draft of an 800- to 1,000-word short story on your chosen outline and character sketches. Then set it aside. Do not attempt to edit it at this time.

Polishing
Your Work

Chapter Eighteen

Rewriting Your Story

Congratulations! You have written the first draft of a short story! Now comes the hard part—rewriting.

I'm not, however, going to ask you to rewrite your story—you're going to rewrite one of mine!

Every story ever written can be modified to change the overall message through rewriting. An editor may ask you to change a character's personality—which, of course, would affect the basic story line. Or, perhaps the editor just wants a different ending—he may have a specific message in mind.

The following are the last three chapters of a 10,000 word mini-novel entitled "Trial by Jury," which I wrote for Christian Liberty Press. First, review my outline and the list of characters, along with their brief sketches. Then, carefully read chapters eight through ten; you are going to rewrite the entire ending.

Working Title: <u>Trial by Jury</u>

Plot Situation: <u>"Judge" Justin, a teenage boy respected for his honest and impartial judgment of others, is asked to settle a dispute between two rival groups of boys; one member is accused of burning down the other group's clubhouse.</u>

Outline

Chapter 1: The Eastchester clubhouse burns down. A member, Toby Berger, believes he saw the arsonist leaving the scene.

Chapter 2: Toby Berger shares the information with his club members.

Chapter 3: The Eastchesters, especially Jason McQueen, accuse Matt Donohue (a member of a rival club known as the Westchesters) of setting the fire.

Chapter 4: "Judge" Justin Powell is called upon to settle the dispute. Justin recommends having a trial with a jury of Matt's peers; both club presidents agree and will act as attorneys.

Chapter 5: Justin Powell is a devout Christian who studies the law and plans to become a lawyer and eventually a judge someday. He arranges for the trial to be held in his basement on Saturday and agrees to preside as judge over the trial.

Chapter 6: Marc Nicholson (friend of Matt's and fellow member of the Westchesters) is convinced of Matt's innocence.

Chapter 7: Marc Nicholson questions Toby Berger (the eyewitness) and seeks to clear Matt's name.

Chapter 8: The day of the trial arrives; a jury of twelve is chosen.

Chapter 9: The trial begins with "Judge" Justin presiding. The two club presidents act as defense and prosecuting attorneys. The accused, the eyewitness, and a number of spectators are present. Jason McQueen falls under suspicion.

Chapter 10: The jurors reach a verdict—"not guilty." Jason disappears. The Eastchesters apologize to Matt and many express an interest in the law. Justin also explains his interest in the law began years before while studying Solomon in Bible class. In the end, he invites interested parties to attend his Bible class to review the writings of Solomon.

Cast of Characters

Primary Characters:

"Judge" Justin Powell: 15 years old, devout Christian, plans to become a lawyer and judge in the future.

Matt Donohue: the accused, 13 years old, member/Westchesters

Toby Berger: eye-witness, 12 years old, member/Eastchesters

Jason McQueen: main accuser, 14 years old, member/Eastchesters

Marc Nicholson: suspects Jason, 12 years old, member/Westchesters

Joe Hampton: president/Westchesters, 14 years old, defense attorney

Steve Winger: president/Eastchesters, 14 years old, prosecuting attorney

Secondary Characters:

(See diagram of courtroom on page 112.)

Tim Donley	*Johnny Carver*
Andrea Hampton	*Stacie Evan*
Sara Marlow	*Alex Robbins*
Shelly Powell	*Joey Carver*
Katy Anderson	*Mike Hampton*
Kevin Moore	

Trial by Jury

by Ruth E. McDaniel

Chapter Eight

Saturday rolled around faster than he would have imagined, and Matt found himself back at Joe Hampton's house. Joe's sister, Andrea, answered the doorbell.

"Matt's here," Andrea called over her shoulder. Then she turned to Matt and smiled. "I'm going to try out for the jury," she said, pointing to the sign taped to the front of Justin's house. It read: "jurors wanted—1 to 5 pm, today—ages 11 through 16, only."

Matt blushed and mumbled, "Well—um—I'll see you there, then."

"Don't worry—it will work out," Andrea said. She moved aside to let her older brother join Matt.

"Well, I think I'm ready," Joe announced as he stepped onto the front porch. He carried a folder filled with notes and copies.

"What's that?" Matt asked, eyeing the folder curiously.

"This is your defense," Joe said, flipping through the numerous pages. "Justin, Steve, and I studied the legal system together—we even went to watch a real trial last week so we'd know what to do. It was pretty interesting and gave us a lot to think about." They walked around the side of Justin's house to the basement entry.

Justin's basement door was propped open, and a sign was taped to it with an arrow pointing inside. It read: Courtroom. A small crowd was gathered at the entrance.

"Follow me," Joe said to Matt, bypassing the group.

"Good luck, Matt," a girl said as they walked by.

Matt turned around and saw Stacie Evan standing with the others. She was in Matt's art class at school. He nodded then hurried to catch up with Joe.

As they entered the basement, Matt looked around with interest. Against the far wall, Justin Powell sat at a wooden table. He was talking to Sara Marlow, one of Steve's neighbors. A solitary chair in front of Justin's desk would be used for witnesses. The "jury box" was split—six chairs were lined up along the left wall, and six chairs lined the right wall. Some of the jury seats were already filled. On the left, Jason McQueen sat in the center with Tim Donley and Kevin Moore on either end. "Justin must be seating them," Matt thought in amusement. Jason didn't look very happy sitting between two members of a rival club.

On the right, the inseparable threesome, Alex and the twins, occupied the first, third, and sixth chairs.

Matt and Joe walked over to a small table on the left, facing Justin and the split jury. "Have a seat," Joe told Matt. "I have to see 'the judge.'"

Matt sat down and glanced to his right. Steve Winger and Toby Berger were seated at another small table facing the bench. They were in a deep discussion and didn't seem to notice that the room was slowly filling up.

"Judge" Justin directed Sara to the vacant jury seat between Jason and Tim. Then he beckoned to the small group at the back of the room. Andrea, Katy, and Shelly Powell came forward with Mike Hampton, Joe's eleven-year-old brother and the youngest member of the Westchesters.

Joe acknowledged the passing group as he rejoined Matt. "It won't be long now. Justin is almost finished seating the jury. The trial will start in a few minutes." He looked up as more people entered the basement. "I'd better take down those signs, or they'll keep coming in."

As Joe left to remove the signs and inform the newcomers that the jury was filled, Marc Nicholson sat down behind Matt.

"Hi, Matt!" Marc looked around the basement. "Wow! This is even beginning to look like a courtroom."

As Justin directed the rest of the jury to their seats, Marc leaned close to Matt and whispered, "Toby's going to feel like hamburger when Joe is finished cross-examining him." He grinned knowingly at Matt, but Joe returned before he could say more.

"Here we go!" Joe said.

Marc sat back in his chair. Matt and Joe turned to face the judge and the jury. Toby ran back to close the basement door and asked the spectators to take a seat. It was time for the trial to begin!

Chapter Nine

"May I have your attention?" RAP! RAP! RAP! Justin banged his gavel on the desk, calling for order in the court.

The room became silent and everyone faced Justin Powell. He set his gavel aside, stood up, and picked up his Bible.

"Since this is just a 'mock' trial, we won't follow every step required in a real court. I'm asking both attorneys to accept the jury—as is."

Joe and Steve nodded in agreement.

"Now, please bow your heads and pray that justice will be served this afternoon." Justin closed his eyes and said, "Lord, I lift up this trial to You and ask for Your divine guidance. Let the truth be known …"

Some foot shuffling to the right of the room made Matt and Joe look sideways. Toby's face was pink, and he hunkered down lower in his seat.

"And, Father," Justin continued, "let me remember Your instructions in Leviticus 19:15, to '… judge your neighbor fairly' when I make decisions in legal cases … Amen!"

Everyone said, "Amen!" and chairs screeched on the tile floor as they all settled more comfortably in their seats. The latest newcomers sat in the remaining chairs and sofas or sat cross-legged on the floor. The basement was filled was friends, neighbors, and classmates.

"First, I'll introduce the jury. Starting on your left: Tim Donley, Andrea Hampton, Sara Marlow, Jason McQueen, Katy Anderson, and Kevin Moore. On your right: John Carver, Stacie Evan, Alex Robbins, Shelly Powell, Mike Hampton, and Joe Carver." Justin looked at the split panel and said, "Jury, do you swear to hear the testimony, fairly and objectively, and try to reach an impartial decision, so help you God?" The jury answered, "We do." Then, Justin turned back to the courtroom.

"Copies of the jury lineup have been given to both attorneys."

Justin looked at Joe and Steve and they nodded.

"Next, the Prosecuting Attorney, Steve Winger, will make his opening statement to the jury." Justin sat down and turned the floor over to Steve.

Picking up his folder of notes, Steve stepped in front of his table and faced Justin and the jury. "Ladies and gentlemen of the jury," Steve began … then stopped when everyone laughed. "Well, you know what I mean," he said, pausing to allow the mood to become more serious. Then he began again. "One week ago today, the Eastchesters' clubhouse burned down. An eyewitness saw the defendant, Matt Donohue, running away from the scene of the crime. We contend that the defendant set the fire."

"That's not true!" Matt cried out in frustration.

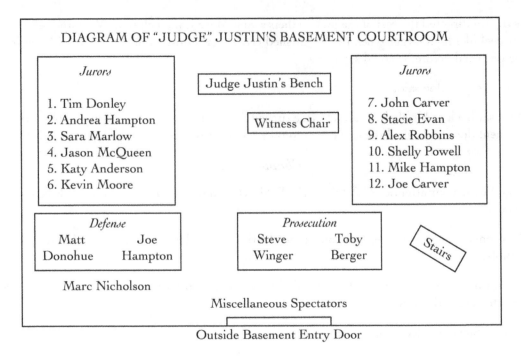

DIAGRAM OF "JUDGE" JUSTIN'S BASEMENT COURTROOM

Judge Justin's Bench

Witness Chair

Jurors

1. Tim Donley
2. Andrea Hampton
3. Sara Marlow
4. Jason McQueen
5. Katy Anderson
6. Kevin Moore

Jurors

7. John Carver
8. Stacie Evan
9. Alex Robbins
10. Shelly Powell
11. Mike Hampton
12. Joe Carver

Defense

Matt Donohue   Joe Hampton

Marc Nicholson

Prosecution

Steve Winger   Toby Berger

Stairs

Miscellaneous Spectators

Outside Basement Entry Door

RAP! RAP! "You'll have your turn, Matt," Justin gently admonished.

"That's all, Your Honor," Steve said, taking his seat.

"At this time, Defense Attorney Joe Hampton will make his opening statement."

Joe stood up and spoke from his place at the table. "My client, Matt Donohue, was asleep in his bed when the fire started. He is innocent of this crime." With that, Joe sat back down.

Justin looked at Steve and said, "Mr. Winger, you may present your witness."

Steve got up. "I call Toby Berger to the witness stand."

Toby walked self-consciously to the empty chair in front of Justin's desk.

Justin stood up and held out the Bible, saying, "Place your left hand on the Bible and raise your right hand." When Toby had complied, Justin continued, "Do you swear to tell the truth, the whole truth, and nothing but the truth, so help you God?"

"I do," Toby mumbled.

"Be seated," Justin instructed, taking his seat as well.

"Now, Mr. Berger," Steve began, noting with satisfaction that the spectators in the courtroom no longer giggled at intervals, "will you tell the court what took place on the morning of the fire?"

Toby cleared his throat and said, "Around two o'clock last Saturday morning, the sound of sirens woke me up. I ran to my bedroom window to see what was happening. Everything seemed all right in the back yard, so I was turning to go to the front of the house when I saw Matt Donohue, wearing a dark, hooded sweat shirt with the hood up, run across my yard and hop over the fence."

The screeching of a chair being pushed back stopped Toby's testimony for a moment. Joe whispered something to Matt, and he settled back, glaring at Toby.

Jason McQueen leaned forward, resting his elbows on his knees, and looked intently at the witness.

"When I got dressed and ran out to the front of the house, I saw that our clubhouse was on fire," Toby continued.

"How do you know it was Matt Donohue in your back yard?" Steve asked.

"There was a full moon that night, and I could see him when he left the shadows. He turned around, once, and looked toward the house. Then he jumped the fence."

"And why would Matt Donohue want to set fire to our clubhouse?" Steve asked.

"He told Jason he was going to get even with him for reporting a foul during a basketball game, two nights before," Toby responded.

"Objection!" Joe interrupted. "That's hearsay, Your Honor."

"Sustained." Toby turned around in confusion, and Justin told him, "You can only repeat what you heard directly."

"No more questions, Your Honor," Steve said as he took his seat.

"Mr. Hampton, do you want to examine this witness?" Justin asked.

"Yes, Your Honor, I certainly do!" Joe glanced at his notes. Then he stood up and walked forward. "Mr. Berger, I'm told your back fence is at least 75 feet away from your window. So, even with a full moon, how could you see my client's face clearly on the night of the fire?"

"Well … I didn't exactly see his features, but, I recognized him anyway."

"If you didn't see his face, how could you recognize him?" Joe asked, stopping two feet in front of Toby.

Toby looked over at Jason, but Joe stepped between them and repeated his question.

"Well … uh … I could tell by his height and the way he moved. It was Matt, all right. And, he had dark hair …"

"Didn't you say the trespasser wore a hooded sweat shirt?"

"Yes, but, you know, they don't cover your hair completely. He had to have dark hair—light or blonde hair would have showed."

"Not if the hood was tied tightly around his face to keep his hair hidden," Joe added. "How tall would you say Matt is?"

"Oh … about 5'9", or 5'10"." Toby's face was pink again.

"Well, I'm 5'10", and I have dark hair, too," Joe pointed out. "Why didn't you think it was me?"

"Because, I recognized the way Matt vaulted over the fence. I've seen him jump hurdles at school dozens of times—that, plus his height and build … well, I just recognized him, that's all!"

Joe leaned toward Toby and said, "I think you saw a trespasser but didn't know who it was, until someone later convinced you it was Matt. Isn't that true?"

"I object!" Jason McQueen yelled.

RAP! RAP! RAP! 'Judge' Justin turned to Jason and said, "Members of the jury are not allowed to speak during a trial."

"But, Matt said …"

"McQueen, please sit back and be quiet!"

"I don't want to be a member of the jury," Jason said angrily. "I want to testify!"

Justin asked Steve and Joe to approach the bench. When they did, Justin said, "This would never be allowed in a real courtroom, but—if you're both in agreement, I can assign Marc Nicholson to replace Jason. Then Jason can testify." Steve agreed.

Joe looked from Jason to Marc. "Well, I was going to use Marc as a character witness, but … okay." Joe turned and motioned for Marc to come forward.

Justin informed everyone of the change, then asked, "Mr. Hampton, have you finished questioning Toby Berger?"

"As soon as he answers my last question, Your Honor." Joe asked Toby, once more, "Isn't it true that you didn't see the trespasser's face clearly and didn't connect him with my client until someone convinced you it was Matt—and, remember, you're still under oath!"

Toby looked over at Steve, then shrugged. "Yes, I guess so."

"I have no further questions, Your Honor."

Toby hurried to the back of the room to sit next to the door, and Steve said, "I call Jason McQueen to the witness stand."

Murmurs accompanied Jason's short walk to the witness chair. Justin held out the Bible and swore Jason in, but he barely heard Jason's mumbled, "I do!"

"Would you tell us, in your own words, what took place on, and just prior to, the morning of the fire?" Steve asked.

Jason sat rigid with hostility. He stared at Matt as he spoke, "Two nights before the fire, Matt shoved me during the basketball game. I went to the referee and reported the foul, and Matt got mad. Later, he said, 'I'll get even with you.' So, when I saw the clubhouse burning and heard the description of the guy who jumped Toby's fence—I put two-and-two together."

"No more questions." Steve looked troubled when he sat down.

Joe approached the witness. "Did anyone else hear this so-called 'threat'?"

"I don't know," Jason shrugged and slumped down in his chair.

"Judge, can I ask the spectators a question?" Joe asked.

Justin's eyebrows drew together. "Well, not during a real trial—but, I guess it's okay here."

Joe turned around and asked, "Were any of you present at the basketball game that night?"

Two boys raised their hands and said, "We played on Jason's team."

"Did either one of you see that 'foul,' or hear a 'threat'?"

They looked at each other, then back at Joe, and shook their heads.

Joe turned to Jason. "But one more thing—where were you when the fire started?"

"What's that supposed to mean?" Jason sat up and glared at Joe as the courtroom erupted in conversation.

RAP! RAP! RAP! RAP! Justin banged his gavel several times before everyone quieted down. Then he told the witness, "Answer the question."

Jason slouched down again and said, "I was asleep!"

"You live on the block behind Toby Berger, and yet, you were at the scene of the fire, fully dressed, shortly after Toby arrived. Isn't that true?"

Jason refused to meet Joe's eyes. "I don't know when Toby got there."

"And can you kindly explain to the court why you appeared at the scene of the fire on a chilly night without a coat or sweat shirt?"

Jason turned to the judge and complained that he was not the one on trial and therefore should not be required to answer such a question. "Very well," said the judge, "I will require the question to be stricken from the record."

"Your Honor, I'm finished with the witness." Joe turned to his chair.

Steve stared thoughtfully at Jason.

"The witness can step down," the judge told Jason. Then he asked Steve, "Does the prosecution have any more witnesses?"

"No, Your Honor."

"Does the defense have any witnesses?"

"No, Your Honor," Joe responded. He whispered to his client, "No need for you to testify, Matt."

Everyone watched as Jason walked to the back of the basement, went outside, and slammed the door behind him. Toby stood staring at the floor.

"Then, it's time for summation," Justin announced.

Chapter Ten

"Mr. Hampton will address the jury first," 'Judge' Justin informed the court.

Joe stood between the twelve jurors and made eye contact with each one of them. Finally, he said, "Members of the jury, you've heard the testimony of a witness who didn't actually see the trespasser's face, and an accuser, who tells of a confrontation on a crowded basketball court that no one else saw or heard." He paused. "The prosecution failed to prove its case. Therefore, you must find my client 'not guilty' of setting fire to the Eastchesters' clubhouse." Joe nodded to Justin, then returned to his seat.

"Is the prosecution ready to address the jury?" Justin asked.

Steve looked up from his notes, glanced at Matt, then looked at the jury. "I have nothing more to say, Your Honor."

Justin spoke directly to the panel, "Normally, the judge would tell the jury to retire from the courtroom so you can deliberate. However, I think it's all right for you to group together, at this end of the basement, while we all step down to the other end.

"First, you must choose a 'foreman'—someone who will speak for you and turn in your verdict. Then, you will deliberate. You must agree 100%—without a reasonable doubt—that the defendant, Matt Donohue, is 'guilty' of setting fire to the clubhouse, or he is 'not guilty' of this crime. Do you understand?"

The jurors nodded.

"All right. I'll be over by the door if you have any questions."

Justin joined Steve, Matt, and Joe as they walked to the farthest wall away from the jury. Some of the spectators opened the door and stepped out into the back yard. Jason was nowhere in sight.

Toby watched as Matt and the others approached him. When they were close enough, he said, "Listen, Matt, I'm sorry about all of this. I really thought it was you—but now ... I must have been wrong."

Matt looked at Toby and started to say something, but he changed his mind, and shrugged, instead. "Okay," he finally muttered.

One of the spectators walked up to Justin and asked, "Aren't you Justin Powell? I heard about you from some of the kids at school. I understand you plan to practice law ... I was really impressed this afternoon. In fact, all of you did a great job. When I first heard about this trial, I thought it was a big joke—but, well, if I'm ever accused of a crime, I'll come to you for help."

"Thanks ... I guess," Justin said, laughing.

"I agree," a fellow student said. "I learned more about how a court of law operates this afternoon than I did all last semester at school."

Just then, Marc Nicholson approached the group.

"Do you have a question, Marc?" Justin asked.

"No. I'm the foreman, and I just wanted to let you know that the jury has reached a verdict."

"Already?" Justin looked at Matt, Steve, and Joe. "Well, tell everybody to come inside—court is back in session."

'Judge' Justin returned to "the bench" as Steve informed the rest of the group that court was reconvening.

Once everyone had taken their seats, Justin rapped the table with his gavel.

"Court is now in session," he said.

The room quieted down, and the spectators leaned forward in anticipation.

Justin looked at Marc and asked, "Has the jury reached a verdict?"

Marc smiled and replied, "We have, Your Honor."

"Will the defendant please rise?" When Matt and Joe stood up, Justin turned to Marc again. "What is your verdict?"

"We find the defendant, Matt Donohue, not guilty of setting fire to the Eastchesters' clubhouse!"

"YAHOO!" "Hooray!" "That's great!" The courtroom erupted in a variety of hoots and well-wishes.

RAP! RAP! Justin smiled at the chaos and said, "The defendant is dismissed, and court is adjourned!"

The jurors surged forward to shake hands with Matt and Joe.

Steve walked over to Matt and held out his hand in a combined gesture of reconciliation and congratulations. "I knew it was going to turn out this way ever since Joe questioned Toby. I should have dug deeper into his story. I'm sorry, Matt. I have a feeling the Eastchesters need to do some soul-searching."

Matt shrugged and shook hands to show his acceptance of Steve's apology. "Just don't let it happen again," he added with a lopsided grin.

Marc pounded Matt on the back and smiled broadly. "What a great afternoon! We should do this more often!"

"Only, the next time, you can be the accused!" Matt replied.

Steve turned to Justin and said, "I really enjoyed studying with you, 'Judge'. In fact, the next time you plan to visit a courtroom, let me know. I'd like to go with you. Suddenly, the law has become fascinating to me."

"I'll do that," Justin agreed.

"You said that you first became interested in the law after reading about King Solomon in the Bible," Steve continued. "Tell me about it."

"Funny you should mention that," Justin said, "My Sunday school class is going to study King Solomon tomorrow morning. Marc and I are in the same room. Maybe you'd like to come with us … you'll even get some material to take home with you."

"Sure! That sounds great. What time should I be here?"

A small voice piped up from behind them, "Can I come, too?" Toby Berger stepped into view with a hopeful look on his face.

"Absolutely!" Justin said, placing a welcoming hand on Toby's shoulder.

Matt looked up with sudden interest. "How about me, too?"

Joe grinned at Justin, who said loudly, "Everyone who would like to study King Solomon at our Sunday school class tomorrow morning—be here by 8:00 a.m.!"

The End

Writing Exercise

Pretend I'm the editor. I like this story, but I'm not sure about the ending. Rewrite the last three chapters for me using one of the following alternative endings:

1. Jason McQueen has a change of heart and confesses to setting fire to the Eastchesters' clubhouse; he blamed it on Matt out of jealousy. Now, he's sorry and wants to make amends.

2. Based on information Marc Nicholson has given him, Joe Hampton accuses Jason McQueen of setting the fire; Jason breaks down on the witness stand and confesses. Jason asks for a second chance, he apologizes to Matt and friends, and he agrees to rebuild the Eastchesters' clubhouse.

3. Choose your own ending.

Chapter Nineteen

Take a Second Look

$\mathcal{R}$emember how I told you that creative writing is fun and exciting? Well, that's true—but, it's also hard work. And now, the hardest job of all begins … proofreading.

Proofreading is simply reading your manuscript and making corrections and improvements. That's what you're going to do with the story you wrote at the end of Chapter Seventeen. Retrieve your story, gather your red pen, pencils, scissors, and clear tape, and let's get to work.

Proofreading with Symbols

Familiarize yourself with the following correction symbols. These symbols are used by editors to proof-read manuscripts they accept. With red pens, they note corrections or insert recommendations between the lines—that is the reason you had to double-space your manuscript. The red corrections are easily seen against the white page when you retype your story.

Symbol	Meaning	Symbol	Meaning
¶	begin a new paragraph	⊙	incorrect punctuation
[	move to the left	sp	spell out (do not abbreviate)
]	move to the right	ℓ lc	use lowercase (lowercase)
ℓ	delete letter(s)	m̲	capitalize
∧	insert in this space	cap ed	(underlined) all CAPS
[ ]	delete this sentence	BF mu	(underlined) **boldface**
◯	misspelled word	X	center
tr	transpose letters or words (sp ace)	ˇ	insert apostrophe
#	insert a space (a#space)	⊙	insert period
eq #	space evenly between words/letters	: ;	insert colon; insert semicolon
⌃	insert a comma	↯ ↯	insert quotation marks
∫	imperfect sentence	del line	~~Delete the entire sentence or paragraph~~
?	unclear	stet	let it stand (i.e., do not change)

Revising Your Manuscript

You should always set your manuscript aside for a few days (This is called "distancing yourself from your story.") so you will be able to view it with a fresh outlook. Now that some time has passed since you wrote your story, the first thing you will do is read it through from beginning to end.

Use the correction symbols shown on the previous page when you begin to proofread. These are the areas you need to pay particular attention to:

1. Does any part of your story sound stiff and awkward? Rewrite those passages until they flow more smoothly.

2. Do your scenes change naturally, or do they seem out of order or out of sequence? Clip those sections out with your scissors and rearrange them. Once they're in the proper sequence, tape them in place. (Scissors and tape are unnecessary if you are able to utilize a word processor for this process.)

3. Does your dialogue sound realistic or artificial? Rewrite it using natural conversation, complete sentences, contractions, and clear language. If it still doesn't sound right, go back and review Chapter Fourteen. Then read your character's dialogue once more. Chances are the problem passage will stand out and you can correct it. If some of the dialogue seems unnecessary, cross it out. Keep your writing tight—only brooks should "babble."

4. Does your story have any awkward words? Read your story out loud and circle cumbersome words (words that make your tongue trip over your teeth) or unclear sentences. Then correct or eliminate them.

5. What about the mechanics of your story? Check your spelling, punctuation, and capitalization; check for "typos" (typing errors).

6. Did you dangle any participles or misplace any modifiers?

7. Did you use any worn-out clichés, similes, or metaphors?

8. Does your story move quickly or slowly?

9. Is your narrative as descriptive as it should be?

10. Are your characters real? Will your readers care about them?

11. Did you use a forceful beginning?

12. Is your climax a turning point for your central character?

13. Do you have a powerful ending?

14. Are your sentence lengths varied?

15. Did you speak in an active rather than a passive voice? Is your character "doing" rather than "receiving" the action? (Active: The dog caught the ball. Passive: The ball was caught by the dog.) Remember, passive voice is boring.

16. Are your sentences too long?

17. Did you follow your plot, outline, and character sketches so you did not meander (or change the cat's gender, by mistake)?

18. Is your story line believable?

19. Does your story make sense?

20. Is your message clear, and does it say what you want it to say?

21. Did you "show" your story and "not tell" it?

22. Finally, do you like your story?

Writing Exercise

1. Now, proofread your story and make appropriate corrections/changes. Then retype your manuscript in the finished form using 8 1/2" x 11" white paper, typed double-space with pica (10 characters per inch) or elite (12 characters per inch), and 1 1/2" margins all around. Don't use an italic or fancy font, but use a standard 12 point font such as Times or Times Roman. Drop down 1/3 of the first page and center your title (all CAPS) and center your byline (your name) directly under the title. Type your name and address in the upper-left-hand corner of the first page, and the approximate number of words in your story in the upper-right-hand corner (to calculate, #10 pica averages 10 words per line with 1 1/2" margins; 25 lines per page equals 250 words per page; multiply the number of pages by 250). On the second through the last pages, type the title in the upper-left-hand corner and your name in the upper-right-hand corner; center your page number in the bottom margin of each page. On the last page, center "The End" following the end of your story (this alerts the editor/reviewer that your story has ended, just in case your ending is unclear).

2. After you have typed your corrected manuscript, proofread it again. Make additional corrections, if needed, and retype it once more.

Note: Repeat the above steps until your manuscript is as perfect as you can make it. Never knowingly release a story to any audience unless it is morally sound and technically accurate in every detail.

Chapter Twenty

Critiques and Copyrights

I've found that one of the most confusing—and often crushing—influences on a new writer is criticism of his work. No one likes to be criticized, and new writers are especially sensitive because they have not built up their skills or confidence. If you are serious about learning the craft of writing, however, you are going to have to learn not only to live with criticism but to seek it out.

Once you write your thoughts on paper and have completed your rough draft, you should begin to view it with a critical eye (follow the proofreading steps in Chapter Nineteen).

Next, you will need to get an outside opinion (and, hopefully, some constructive criticism). But you don't want just anyone to review your manuscript.

The following is a list of critique or review suggestions that I've used since I began to write professionally. They have helped me receive acceptances from a wide variety of publishing houses. Perhaps they can help you, too.

1. Try to find a published writer to review your work.

If you don't know any published writers in your area, I recommend asking an English teacher, your pastor, or a local writers' group to look your work over. *The Christian Writers' Market Guide* (available in most Christian bookstores) has a list of writing groups located throughout the United States; critiquing is a regular function of these groups. Check with your local library; most libraries sponsor writing groups—or know of some. Also, many writing associations have "Round Robins"—these are writers who review each other's work through the mail. Call the English Department of your local Christian college for more recommendations.

2. Make sure your reviewer is qualified to judge your work.

Not only should your critic know *how* to write, he must also know *what* to write in this day and age. That is why I recommend trying to find a reviewer whose work has been recently published. Your story must appeal to today's reader. So, you will need guidance from someone who is familiar with current writing styles, as well as plotting, vivid dialogue, forceful beginnings, and powerful endings.

3. There is safety in numbers.

Unless the first evaluation strikes you as right and reasonable, try to obtain two or more opinions. One critic's recommendation might be based on personal preference rather than sound writing advice.

4. Never ask a friend or relative for a review.

I would not even mention this, but new writers continue to tell me that their families think their work is brilliant. Now if that family happens to own a publishing house, all's well and good. Otherwise … consider the source and their bias.

5. Walk softly in writers' groups.

As I said earlier, writers' groups are great places to have your work critiqued—within reason. If the group's writers have been published and have some expertise in creative writing, then you have struck gold. Most published writers genuinely try to help novices break into print. It's flattering to be asked for advice by a new writer. However, study their comments carefully. Remember, each writer has his own voice; don't change your style to match his. Also, don't confuse encouragement with constructive criticism. Some established writers are simply incapable of criticizing someone else's work.

6. Take up permanent residency at the library.

There is no substitute for reading good literature. A person who does not read avidly will never become a good writer. As you read, you are subconsciously absorbing grammar, plotting, dialogue, presentation, composition—in other words, you are gathering knowledge needed to create your own work. But, don't limit your studies to either the classics or the latest novels. A complete writing education includes both. The classics will provide insight into subjects and styles that have universal and ageless appeal, while current works will instruct you in contemporary trends, tone, and story lines. Then, read critical reviews of those works. Write your own reviews of the books you have read. What did you like or dislike about them? How did the author plot, build the story, handle his characters and dialogue?

By the way, while you are at the library, make friends with the librarians. They are well-read and can tell you which subjects are the most popular with today's readers. One of those subjects just might develop into your next story.

7. Should you pay for professional editing and critiquing?

There are legions of publishers and individuals advertising these services in writing/literary magazines. However, few new writers can afford them. You can receive hands-on editing in any English composition class and cover a lot more material for the same amount of money or less. But this is a decision each writer must make for himself.

I advise caution in selecting professional critiquing. Once again, try to determine the qualifications of the reviewer before sending your story and your check. To my knowledge, no license is required to become a critic. You might be better off using your local writing group or attending Christian writers' conferences.

8. Write continuously.

The old adage is true, "Practice makes perfect." The more you write, the better you will become—that is, if you have acquired good writing skills and you read voraciously. Never stop reading, learning, or writing, and your abilities will improve.

9. Take that critique under advisement.

View all criticism of your work dispassionately. Don't let your emotions cloud your judgment. Very few stories are flawless. Be open and honestly evaluate the reviewer's recommendations. Then, rewrite, rewrite, rewrite! The end result could be your first byline (publication under your name).

Copyright Law

Did you know that once you write a story, it's yours—legally? Published or unpublished, you own the copyright to that story, and you don't even have to register it with the copyright office in Washington, D.C.

The change in copyright laws which went into effect on January 1, 1978, states that you (the owner/author) are given the exclusive right to reproduce the copyrighted work in any tangible medium of expression (copies, public performance, anthologies, publications, etc.). This right lasts throughout your lifetime, plus seventy years after your death.

How do you let the general public know that you are the legal owner? By typing the copyright notice at the top of your manuscript.

1. the copyright symbol = © (*c* in a circle), or the word *copyright*[34]

2. the year your work was completed

3. your name

Example: © 1995 Ruth E. McDaniel

If your story is published in a magazine, it will be copyrighted twice—once under your name and once by the magazine. Most magazines are copyrighted. You will find the copyright notice on the masthead[35] inside the front cover.

Note: Ideas, names, titles, short phrases, concepts, and slogans cannot be copyrighted.

It is illegal for anyone to use copyrighted material in any form without the author's permission (see the "public domain" and "fair use" exceptions below). But what if someone does? Once your work is published, you will have to face that possibility; in fact, it happened to me. In that case, you can hire a lawyer and take the violator to court, or talk to him, let him know he's broken the law, and accept his promise not to do it again. I chose the latter.

---

34. For most fonts, the copyright symbol is made on a personal computer by pressing the *alt* key and typing 0169 in Microsoft® Word or the *option* key and the letter *g* simultaneously on the Macintosh®.

35. This is a box or section printed in each issue of a newspaper or magazine giving the names of the publishers, owners, and editors; the location of their offices; subscription rate; and so forth.

According to the U.S. Copyright Office, prior to 1978 copyright was secured either on the date a work was published—with a copyright notice—or on the date an unpublished work was registered. In either case, the copyright endured for a period of *28 years* from the date it was secured. During the last year of this period, the copyright was eligible for renewal for another *28 years*, for a total of *56 years*. However, the **Copyright Act of 1976** extended the renewal term to *47 years* for copyrights that were still in effect, for a total of *75 years*. On October 27, 1998, **Public Law 105–298** further extended existing copyrights an additional 20 years, providing a renewal term of *67 years*, for a total of *95 years*. Otherwise, a work is considered to be in the **public domain**—which makes it available for free use by the general public. Of course, the original author must be credited if any part of his work is used. Not to do so would be considered **plagiarism**.

You should also know that a work that is created on or after January 1, 1978, is automatically protected from the moment of its creation and is ordinarily given a term enduring for the *author's life* plus an additional *70 years* after the author's death. Works originally created before January 1, 1978, but not published or registered by that date have been automatically brought under the statute and are now given federal copyright protection. The duration of copyright in these works will generally be computed in the same way as for works created on or after January 1, 1978—the life of the author plus 70 years.

What if you just want to quote something from the works of a modern author? The copyright law allows for "fair use," which is the right to include brief quotes from another's work without his permission. However, the author must be identified and credited. When in doubt, write to the author's publishing house and ask for the author's written permission.

To register your work, you must mail two copies of your manuscript, a $30 payment made out to "Register of Copyrights," and registration forms (**Form TX** or **Short Form TX** *and* **Form CON**) to:

> Library of Congress
> Copyright Office
> 101 Independence Avenue, S.E.
> Washington, D.C. 20559-6000

One final comment is worth mentioning. If you are having difficulty finding out if a writing selection is in the public domain, you can write to the Library of Congress and request that they perform a "Copyright Search/Copyright Status Report." You need to give them the *author's name*, *title* of the writing selection, original *copyright date* (if known), approximate *year of publication* or *creation*, *registration number* (if known), and any other identifying information. This special service has an administrative fee of $75 per hour. If you need to take advantage of this service, contact the Library of Congress directly or make a request on-line at <http://www.copyright.gov/forms/search_estimate.html>.

Chapter Twenty-one

Advice for New Writers

What next? Take a deep breath, because it's time to submit your short story (or poem or article) to an editor for possible publication.

Yes! You can do it! The world needs Christian writers—and that's you! Age does not matter!

How, exactly, do you go about it? Read on.

I have been writing professionally since 1992. In that time, I have received several hundred acceptances for short stories, novelettes, poems, and articles. In addition, I have given nearly 200 readings and written and published 20 chapbooks. For that reason, I am often asked to teach writing workshops.

Invariably, the first question asked at each workshop is: "How did you get started?" Then, in rapid succession … "How do you know what to write?", "How do you find markets?", "How often do you write?", "What type of equipment do you use?", "Will you help me get published?", "Should I send a cover letter with my manuscript?", etc. I will answer each question, as space permits.

How did you get started?

Due to illness in the family, I took an early retirement from an administrative position at Washington University in May 1991. I had always wanted to write professionally and now I needed an avocation I could pursue within my home while I cared for my husband. So, in early 1992, I wrote an article about the disease that was attacking him (Multiple Sclerosis), and how it affected each member of our family. I sent a copy of this article to the Multiple Sclerosis Society, and they published it in their next newsletter.

Then, I noticed that a local senior newspaper featured a poetry column. I sent some of my poems to the editor, and she began publishing one in each issue. When I asked if she could use some freelance articles, she agreed to review them. She has since published a number of my holiday and specialty articles.

A few months later, I began submitting short stories to Christian publications and my work was accepted by several of them. (There are scores of publishers who need short articles for Sunday school take-home papers. That is a great place to start.)

The experience gained from these first acceptances gave me the confidence to expand my markets.

How do you know what to write?

As we discussed in Chapter Eight, there is an endless supply of subjects to write about (review Chapter Eight for specifics).

What type of writing do you aspire to? Do you want to write poetry, short stories, humor, articles … or all of the above? If you hope to write for a certain publication, editors have definite needs; get samples of their publications and their guidelines before submitting your work to them. Local newspapers can always use timely articles about the community or holidays. Christian publishing houses need Bible-based stories and devotionals for various age groups. Professional journals want related, well-researched essays and articles. Most magazines can use humorous fillers.

One objective is to find out what the needs are and write to fill them. The second option is to write spontaneously and try to find a market afterward.

How do you find markets?

In answer #1, I shared how I found my early markets. In addition, examine your local newspaper and contact the editors listed. If at all possible, attend writers' workshops and conferences in your local area and obtain market information directly from the editors and instructors. Review magazines at your local library and send for guidelines (enclose a one paragraph request, plus an SASE—that's a self-addressed-stamped-envelope) to the editor at the address on the masthead located in the front of the publication.

Purchase *The Christian Writers' Market Guide* (available in Christian bookstores); it will give you invaluable information about submission requirements, payments, etc. But you will still need to send for the latest guidelines before you submit. You can easily recover the cost of the book with your first sale.

Try to find a publication that matches your writing style. That means you will have to read lots of sample copies, but it will save you time and money in the long run.

Submit to the small publishers at first; don't try to break into the large markets (*Reader's Digest*, *The Atlantic*, etc.) until your writing skills match their needs.

Subscribe to writing magazines and poetry journals. Most offer market columns with updated information.

Don't be discouraged if you receive mostly rejection slips at first; even famous writers had 90%+ rejection rates when they started out. If your story is well-written, and if you follow the guidelines exactly, you will eventually find a market. Be persistent and resubmit (clean copies) to the next publisher. (Don't submit the same story to more than one editor at a time.)

These are the steps I've taken to achieve my sales. If it works for me, it will work for you, too.

How often do you write?

Daily. Don't groan and start making excuses—you can write daily, too. I keep pen and paper in every room in the house and jot notes continuously. When I'm watching television, I write. When I sit at the kitchen table with my morning coffee, I write. When relaxing on the porch, I write. And in between writing—I read. Reading helps to improve my writing and provides ideas and inspiration for future compositions. For example, when I read stories about vacations, it may remind me of unusual events which took place on one of my own trips. Or, a particular word in a poem may inspire me to create a verse around that word, etc.

You say you can't find time to write because you are too busy? Remember, I'm a writer, a mother, a grandmother, and a caregiver, too. "Where there's a will, there's a way"—if you are serious about writing, you will make time for it. Dancers, gymnasts, singers, and musicians practice every day to hone their craft; serious writers must do the same.

What type of equipment do I need?

To begin with, all you really need is a typewriter. I started with an electric typewriter and bought a word processor with my first big check. I'll purchase a computer soon, since many editors want IBM-compatible discs instead of paper manuscripts.

I recently purchased a small personal copier to save time and money (I was making daily trips to the copy center). That is one of the best investments I have made so far.

Since I publish my own chapbooks (these are 5 1/2" x 8 1/2", stapled, paper-back books), I've purchased the usual assortment of office hardware, plus a drawing board, long stapler, and paper cutter.

Another essential item is a postage scale. This has reduced my frequent visits to the Post Office.

As the payments arrive, I invest them in equipment and supplies to make my job easier. You don't have to have state-of-the-art equipment in order to be published, but the better the tools, the better the quality of your manuscript, and the faster you can sell it.

Will you help me get published?

What new writers are really asking is for me to act as their agent, so they don't have to spend the time, trouble, and money seeking their own markets. Frankly, I'd love to have someone provide these services for me, as well. But most writers don't have that luxury. (Agents seek you out when you are famous; by then, you don't need them.)

There is no substitute for hard work, and there are no short cuts to publishing. Each writer must spend the necessary time studying publications to find one that matches his work. Then, he must send for guidelines and submit his manuscripts as required. Marketing is a necessary step in this learning process. By working directly with publishers, new writers develop a sense of editorial needs and improve their skills.

Should I send a cover letter with my manuscript?

Yes. A one-page cover letter will suffice. The following format is acceptable:

Your Address

Date

Editor's full name
Name of Publication
Address
City, State, Zip

Dear (editor's name):

Thank you for sending a sample of (Name of Publication), along with your guidelines. I am submitting an unpublished short story entitled (your title). I'm offering first rights for this story (or reprint rights, if you've already sold the story—in that case, name the first publisher and the date the story was published).

(In this section, you can give a brief explanation of why you think this story would appeal to the publication's readers).

(If you have any published works, this is where you would list them; otherwise, just skip this paragraph; you don't want to call attention to your inexperience. If the editor wants more information, he will contact you.)

A self-addressed-stamped-envelope (or SASE) is enclosed; no need to return the manuscript (be sure to keep the original yourself; send clear copies only to editors). Thank you for your consideration. I look forward to hearing from you.

Sincerely,

Your Name

(Area Code) Phone Number

All right—it is time to take the plunge! You have studied and worked hard to produce a marketable story. If you have the desire to see your work in print, you are ready for the next step.

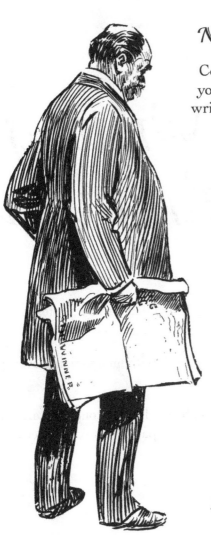

Now You Are a Writer!

Congratulations! You made it to the end of the textbook, which means you have completed all of the writing exercises and you have actually written a short story.

- Did you find it stimulating, inspiring, exciting?

- Did you tap into your imagination?

- Did you try to write words that will make an impact on people's lives?

- Did you have fun?

- Was it a great adventure for you?

In the beginning, I told you to think of your words as wild horses. Did you tame them?

I truly hope you will continue to write. As I said earlier, there is a great need for more Christian writers to help spread God's message throughout the world. Listen closely—is He knocking at your heart? Make the commitment to write for Him. Keep writing and praying and submitting ... and writing and praying and submitting....

May God bless you!

Appendix

Letter Writing Techniques

Recently, I was talking to the administrator of a local bank. She had heard that I was a professional writer and expressed great admiration for my craft.

"How do you do it?" she wanted to know. "I can't even write a business letter without agonizing over it for hours … sometimes days."

I was not shocked by this disclosure; I have heard the same comments from all age groups in various levels of authority. There is something about putting your thoughts down on paper that causes certain people to experience anxiety. It does not have to be that way, however.

"Can you use the telephone?" I asked.

"Of course," she said, looking confused.

"Then, pretend you're talking on the telephone. Visualize the person you want to write to and type the words you would say to him. It's that easy."

She smiled and nodded uncertainly. It was obvious she did not believe me. However, it's true. Here, we will cover letter-writing techniques—ways to improve the physical appearance, the structure, and the content of your letters.

Appearance

Whether you are writing to an editor or to a friend, type your letter. It is neater and more readable, and you will save on postage (you can say more using less paper). Your thoughts will flow smoothly; it is easier to organize your thoughts when you type them out. Your friend will appreciate the time and effort you took. As for editors, first impressions begin with your letter. Neatness, style, sincerity, and correctness make a big impact. An editor will be more inclined to take your work seriously if your letter is presented well.

Don't use onion-skin paper (too thin) or erasable paper (smears too easily). Use a good quality, 20-lb. weight, 8 1/2" x 11", white, bond paper; you do not have to buy expensive stationery or letterhead. Plain white paper is less distracting to the reader. Avoid tinted, decorated, or odd-sized paper.

Fold the letter in thirds and mail it in a standard, white #10 business envelope.

Use a standard size font—pica (#10) or elite (#12). Script typefaces are difficult to read and inappropriate for correspondence. Fancy typeface or handwritten letters will identify you as an amateur.

Business letters should be limited to one page whenever possible. A letter to a friend can run on for several pages, as long as it's interesting—and, as long as you avoid the "ME-ME SYNDROME" ... that is, the tendency to dwell on yourself. There's nothing quite as boring as receiving a letter from someone who talks about himself continuously and forgets to ask what's happening in your life.

Your margins depend on the size of the letter: the shorter your letter, the wider the margins, and vice versa. However, your margins must never be smaller than 1 1/2".

Your letter should be typed single-spaced with double-spacing between paragraphs unless it's extremely short. In that case, double-space to center it more neatly on the page.

Structure

The most common letter formats are *Block Style* and *Semi-Block Style*. Block style is my favorite because it's simple: all parts of the letter begin at the left margin. There are no indentions. Study the following example.

Block Style Letter

234 Jollibee Avenue
Jollibeeshive, USA 60210

Date

Mr. John Doe, Editor
Light the Way Magazine
123 Any Street
Anyplace, USA 12345

Dear Mr. Doe:

In reply to your request for a sample of my work, I've enclosed a copy of an article I wrote on nursing homes that was recently published in *Golden Years Magazine*.

Please don't hesitate to contact me if you need additional samples. I look forward to hearing from you.

Sincerely,

Ruth E. McDaniel
(001) 002-0003

Semi-Block Style Letter

In the semi-block style format, the return address, the date, a reference or subject line, the complimentary close, and identification line are typed on the right side of the page. The inside address, salutation, and paragraphs are blocked, flush with the left-hand margin, and the first line of each paragraph is indented five spaces.

---

234 Jollibee Avenue
Jollibeeshive, USA 60210

Date

Miss Jane Smith
123 Any Street
Anyplace, USA 12345

Dear Ms. Smith:

Subject: Confirmation of 8/20/95

I am pleased that you have agreed to speak on "Interviewing and Writing Profiles" at the Christian Writers' Conference in St. Louis, Missouri, on October 20, 1995.

Your presentation is scheduled to last approximately forty-five minutes. I have arranged for a slide projector and operator, as requested.

I am excited about your participation. I expect a sizable group, and I know they will enjoy your presentation. I look forward to seeing you.

Sincerely,

Ruth E. McDaniel
(001) 002-0003

Indented Style Letter

Of course, you are free to vary these formats. For instance, I recently wrote a letter to the editor of our daily newspaper in response to an article I'd read.[36] Because the letter ran two pages, I indented the first sentence of each paragraph and eliminated the double-spacing between paragraphs in order to shorten the length:

---

36. This letter was published in the editorial section of the *St. Louis Post-Dispatch* on June 24, 1995.

---

234 Jollibee Avenue
Jollibeeshive, USA 6021

June 11, 1995

"Letter From the People" Editor
St. Louis Post-Dispatch
900 North Tucker Blvd.
St. Louis, MO 63101-1099

The article entitled, "Disability Aid for Children," about Deborah Schaefer on page one of the June 11, 1995 edition could have been written about me twenty years ago. I, too, had three hyperactive, attention-deficit-disorder sons exactly the same ages as Schaefer's. However, I didn't have government financial aid (SSI) to help solve the problem. I didn't need it—and neither does Schaefer. As a Christian, a mother, and a taxpayer, I feel the need to offer her an alternative solution. Common sense, love, discipline, and the Bible saw me through the rough times, and they can help Schaefer and others like her:

—Eliminate all sugar, especially candy, and caffeine products;
—Closely monitor or eliminate television viewing, especially programs with lots of action as these stimulate their hyperactivity;
—Supply rocking chairs for each child; they can't sit still and this provides them with an acceptable outlet;
—Daily, take them bike riding, jogging, on picnics at the park close to the playground—encourage anything that involves muscle-usage; this wears them out and better prepares them for sleep;
—Keep prescription drugs to a minimum—eliminate them, if possible; most hyperactives don't require heavy drugs, and the side effects can be harmful, both physically and mentally;
—Don't take them shopping; baby-sit-exchange with friends/neighbors if you don't have family support;
—Hug, kiss, and tell your sons you love them as often as you can; they need to know they're loved in spite of their problems;
—Pray with them daily; listen to their fears and concerns. If you have no spouse, ask the church pastor to get involved. The boys need a strong male role model;
—Discipline them. "If you spare the rod, you'll spoil the child" (Proverbs 13:24). A mild spanking along with being sent to bed helps the younger boys. Other disciplinary actions include no TV, no visits or phone calls to/from friends, etc. On the other hand, reward good behavior.
—"Train up a child in the way he should go, and when he is old he will not depart from it" (Proverbs 22:6). Whatever values or lack of values you implant now will surface later and guide their lives.

How Schaefer handles her children at this age prepares them for manhood. If she follows the suggestions listed above, I can assure her they will grow up to be law-abiding, hard-working, happy men who will fit into society. I have three sons to prove it.

Sincerely,

Ruth E. McDaniel
(001) 002-0003

I urge all Christian writers to submit letters to the editors of secular newspapers and magazines and share the Word of God. It's especially important in this fast-paced society to guide people back to the Bible. Even a liberal newspaper will publish biblical truths if they're presented well; the previous letter attests to that.

Content

Now that you know what type of paper, typefaces, and format to use, it is time to focus on content.

Personal letters are the easiest ones to write because they're written to friends and family—people who won't judge you by what you say … or will they? As I pointed out earlier, if you have a tendency to prattle on about yourself and neglect to ask about your reader's life, health, or activities (remember the "ME-ME SYNDROME"?), your letters will not be as well-received as you think. By all means, tell about your latest happenings, but do not become so self-focused that you can't see beyond your own life.

Letter-writing is an art and follows certain techniques. As in creative writing, the style of your letter should reveal your personality. The tone of your letter will reflect your attitude and thoughts, exactly the way that the tone of your voice mirrors your mood. If you write in a condescending or angry manner, it will be obvious to the reader. Nor can you hide behind artificial words and false "warmth." Be sincere and honest.

Whether it is a formal or informal letter, always use good English, colorful nouns and active verbs. Try to make your letters as interesting and to-the-point as possible. Vary the length of your sentences and paragraphs. The correct salutation, complimentary close, and signature depends on your relationship with the addressee and the content of the letter. If you're writing to a friend, "Dear Bill," and "Love … Sue," is okay. A formal letter, however, would begin "Dear Dr. Doe," or "Dear Ms. Smith," and close, "Sincerely," or "Very truly yours … Ruth E. McDaniel."

Your first sentence should prepare the reader for the rest of the communication. As in writing articles, the leading sentence and paragraph should set the stage and grab the reader, informing them of what is to follow.

> **Example:** "Are you aware that the Spotted Owl is in danger of becoming extinct?"

The body of the letter should follow an interesting, local pattern. If there is a sequence of events, they should be listed in consecutive order.

> **Example:** "This all came about because …" (a) describe the history of the owl species, (b) state the beginning of the loss of habitat, (c) name the current crisis that's endangering the Spotted Owl.

The last sentence should summarize and reinforce the first sentence and the ensuing paragraphs.

> **Example:** "Won't you help us save the Spotted Owl from becoming extinct? Your contribution will make a difference. Thank you so much for you interest and financial assistance."

The following exemplifies a poorly written letter:

Joseph M. Smith, M.D.
123 Maple Street
St. Louis, MO 63111

Dear Joseph M. Smith, M.D.:

How I wish I could come to your seminar and give a talk on "How to Write." It sounds like a really good seminar. I would really like to meet you and the other fine doctors.

But, I've accepted a gig at another conference for that week. They pay better, too. (Just joking!)

Hope you think of me when you start making plans again.

Cordially,

Ruth E. McDaniel
(001) 002-0003

Dr. Smith would definitely remember this letter—adversely. The return address and the date are missing from the top of the letter. The salutation is incorrect. The first paragraph uses poor grammar, poor sentence structure, and repetition. The second paragraph uses slang and inappropriate humor. The final paragraph is incomplete, and the complimentary close is incorrect and too formal.

The following is a more acceptable version:

---

234 Jollibee Avenue
Jollibeeshive, USA 60210

Date

Joseph M. Smith, M.D.
123 Maple Street
St. Louis, MO 63111

Dear Dr. Smith:

I received your gracious invitation to speak at the upcoming medical seminar. It's an intriguing idea, bringing in a professional writer to teach physicians how to express themselves in a way that laymen can understand.

Several months ago, however, I accepted another speaking engagement at the Annual Writers' Conference scheduled on September 18.

I'm sorry I'll miss meeting you and your group. I hope you will keep me in mind for the next year's medical seminar.

Sincerely,

Ruth E. McDaniel
(001) 002-0003

Writing Exercise

1. Rewrite the poorly written letter in your own style. Don't forget to follow the basic rules for writing business letters. Keep it short, to the point, and sincere.

2. Write a letter to the editor of a newspaper, magazine, or newsletter regarding a topic of interest to you. Try to include Christian principles in your letter.

Reference List

Bibles

The Holy Bible: King James Version.

Holy Bible, New International Version © 1984; International Bible Society. Used with permission of Zondervan Publishing House.

New American Standard Bible © 1973; The Lockman Foundation.

Literature Cited

Defoe, Daniel. 1942. *The Life and Adventures of Robinson Crusoe.* NY: The Saalfield publishing Co.

Dickens, Charles. 1963. *Oliver Twist.* NY: Airmont Books.

Felleman, Hazel, ed. 1936. *The Best Loved Poems of the American People.* NY: Doubleday and Co., Inc.

Smith, Elwyn Allen. 1948. *Men Called Him Master.* PA: The Westminster Press.

Williams, Oscar, ed. 1952. *Immortal Poems.* NY: Washington Square Press/Simon and Schuster, Inc.

Reference Works

Kellerman, Dana F., ed. 1981. *The Living Webster Encyclopedic Dictionary of The English Language.* Delair Publishing Co., Inc.

Strunk, William, Jr. 1979. *The Elements of Style.* NY: MacMillan Publishing Co., Inc.

Venolia, Jan. 1988. *Write Right.* CA: Ten Speed Press.

Zinsser, William. 1980. *On Writing Well.* NY: Harper & Row.

Resources

Bond, Jill. 1997. *Writing to the Glory of God.* MD: Homeschool Press.

Meeter, Merle. 1972. *Literature and the Gospel.* PA: Presbyterian and Reformed Publishing.

Schaeffer, Francis A. 1973. *Art and the Bible.* IL: InterVarsity Press.

Stuart, Sally E. 1995. *The Christian Writers' Market Guide.* CA: Joy publishing.